# MINIMAL

*For Simple & Sustainable Living*

# MINIMAL

## *For Simple & Sustainable Living*

Laurie Barrette and
Stéphanie Mandréa

Translated by J. C. Sutcliffe

AMBROSIA

# Contents

# Food

# Beauty & health

# Family

# Introduction

If you are holding this book in your hands, then you, like us, are probably keen to adopt a simpler way of life, at a slower pace, more in harmony with nature. This is a step in the right direction in the process of change.

Our lifestyle hasn't always been the way it is today. Before we dive into the real meat of this book, we'd like to tell you a bit about how we got here. Perhaps our journey will inspire you.

## Who are we?

We are two good friends, who met in high school, and who share an interest in natural foods and products. The more we delved into the topic, the more aware we became of all the harmful agents in our cleaning and beauty products. So we decided to start making our own. If we could bake muffins, why not make our own deodorant, our own moisturizer, or our own laundry soap? A whole world opened up to us!

(At this point, you might be wondering about the connection between all of these homemade products and the famous bread bag our company is known for in Quebec. We'll get to that shortly…)

Bea Johnson's book *Zero Waste Home* was another motivating factor in our change of lifestyle. To this day, we consider it the trigger for our desire to reduce our consumption and ecological footprint even further. When we realized how much waste we generated on a daily basis, our decision to do our part really took hold. At first, the goal of zero waste (being able to fit a year's worth of garbage into a Mason jar) was scary, because it seemed simply unattainable. However, we began by taking baby steps, and those steps gradually grew bigger.

At that time, reusable items weren't readily available, so we had to improvise. Walking to the bakery with a pillowcase in hand to carry the bread, an *aha* moment occurred: Why not create a bread bag with several uses? If making one small change could inspire other people to shift to sustainable living, then we decided our contribution would be to produce this bag.

We initially started our business for fun, without any serious expectations, but then quickly realized that there were a lot of people like us out there — people who aspired to change and were seeking better ecological alternatives to the plastic bag. Starting from one reusable bread bag, *Dans le sac* became a platform for hints and tips on zero waste and minimalism, bringing together a community who were curious about — and motivated to try — a different lifestyle.

## Inspiring — not judging

During the writing of this book, we both became mamas. The great adventure of motherhood has inspired us to rethink our priorities. Our motivation has been renewed, and we want to spend time enjoying the days with our children, showing them the importance of taking care of our planet.

Rather than get hung up on labels like "zero waste" or "minimalist," which come off as judgemental and critical, we simply want to inspire you to move toward a more sustainable lifestyle yourself and give you the tools you need to do it at your own pace and in a way that works for you. We are certainly not perfect ourselves! Over the years, we have enjoyed discovering this world without ever feeling deprived, and we want this to come across in this book.

Because everyday life is not always as flawless as the curated versions we see on Pinterest or Instagram, we have scattered "Real Life" tips throughout the chapters of *Minimal*. This is our way of compromising and finding balance. You will also find our top tricks, recipes, and inspirations, which we hope will make you want to accompany us on this sustainable-living journey.

Happy reading!
*Laurie & Stéphanie*

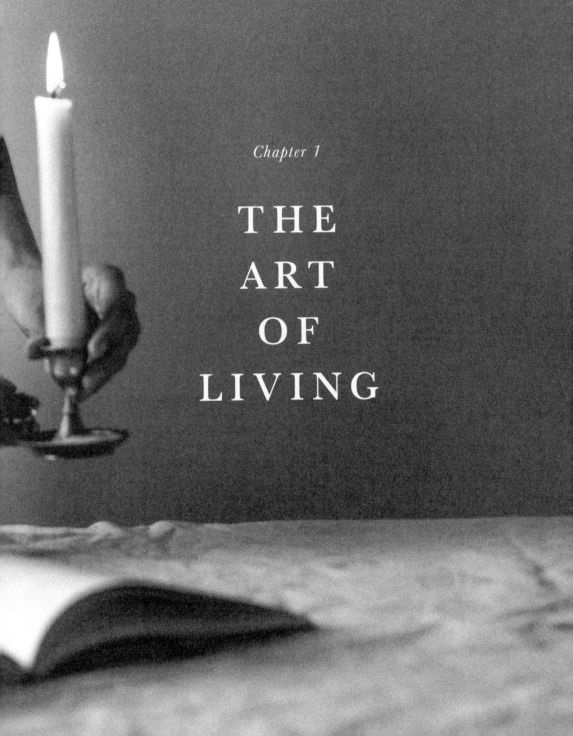

Chapter 1

# THE
# ART
# OF
# LIVING

"HAPPINESS IS NOT
SOMETHING READY-MADE.
IT COMES FROM YOUR
OWN ACTIONS."

Dalai Lama

# Simple living

Have you ever noticed how it's usually the simple things in life that delight us the most? As soon as we strip away the unnecessary elements of our lives and allow ourselves more quality time, we experience contentment. Simplicity can truly make us feel awesome.

## What does simplicity mean to us?

For us, simplicity is bringing things back to basics, taking the time to cook a nice meal, read a book, or even just go for a walk outside. In a world where we are always trying to outdo ourselves, a world in which we are constantly bombarded with advertising and information, it is crucial that we know how to switch off in order to connect better with ourselves, other people, and nature.

Furthermore, it's been proven that neither possessions nor money make us happy. The happiest people are the ones who spend more time with family or friends, who spend time outside, and who take care of themselves.

Paring down the excess allows us to concentrate our energies on the essentials and to reassess our priorities in order to simplify our day-to-day lives. This might look like dropping certain engagements we find burdensome, or developing the ability to say no. We need to stop agreeing to do things just to please other people, and instead learn to respect our limits. Achieving a balanced life and having enough time for ourselves inevitably means putting ourselves before other people.

This might seem selfish, but if it's a choice made for the right reasons, we naturally become more in harmony with ourselves and others.

Each of us has 24 hours in every day. We simply need to make intelligent choices about how to spend them. Even though we run our business, which brings a lot of obligations, we know the importance of setting aside time in our schedules for a yoga class or coffee with friends. This, in essence, is simplicity: taking the time to truly live in the present moment. We guarantee that it will make you more productive in your work, and will improve your mood.

**A STEP IN THE RIGHT DIRECTION**

Over the next week, ask yourself what you could cut from your schedule to make more space for your favourite activities or even for rest. But beware! It's not simply about replacing one task with another; rather, it's about making spaces in your day to leave room for life's little surprises.

# Minimalism

Living more simply and becoming more minimalist does not have to mean getting rid of all your possessions and living in a white room with no furniture. Far from it! Each person has to find the pace and balance that suits them.

Our current rate of consumption is so way out of whack with our needs that soon we will require the equivalent of three planets to meet the needs of future generations. Resisting this norm of consumption that drives us to constantly seek more material goods in order to paper over whatever we are missing inside, a minimalist way of life promises to free us of mental burdens so we can focus on the important things. It's also key to remember not to value material goods over human experiences.

In discussions on minimalism, you may often hear a certain term repeated: *intention*. Being intentional means being attentive to the present moment and living in harmony with it. On a day-to-day basis, living with intention is a useful way to avoid mental overload, as well as to be more aware — and more appreciative — of our surroundings. Thus simplicity inevitably brings with it a sense of mindfulness, and anchors us in the "now."

In these pages we will explore the basics of a minimalist life, built on principles of self-control and decluttering. When we reduce our possessions it helps us differentiate desires from real needs so that, ultimately, we make better decisions as consumers.

**FIVE QUESTIONS TO ASK BEFORE YOU BUY OR RECEIVE ANYTHING**

- Do I really need it?
- Can I repair the one I already own?
- Can I buy it used?
- Can I obtain it from a local company?
- Can I politely refuse?

# REFUSE

## REDUCE

### REUSE

RECYCLE

ROT

# Zero waste

Voluntary simplicity and minimalism are inextricably linked with the new trend toward zero waste, because they all focus on a more sustainable lifestyle. Zero waste, which is more pragmatic than the other two movements, is inspired by five golden rules: refuse, reduce, reuse, recycle, rot. It aims to decrease the amount of waste we produce and to have us question our consumption habits and the life cycle of the products we consume.

## Getting started

Just hearing the words "zero waste" is enough to strike fear into some people's hearts. When starting out it's important to remember that you are not obliged to make enormous sacrifices or live like a monk. You can simply carry on doing everything you love while trying to alter some of your consumer behaviours — in other words, reduce the amount of waste you produce. Whether it's starting to cook more so that you buy fewer processed packaged foods or making your own cleaning products, every action counts. Change starts with yourself, through small actions taken at home or in the workplace.

Striving for zero waste means noticing your behaviour, examining your consumption, and addressing environmental issues.

This book provides food for thought and some practical solutions so you can take charge of your consumption and habits without beating yourself up and going to extremes. Once again, the aim is not to induce guilt or transform you into the perfect zero-waste disciple, but rather to help you live more in harmony with nature and yourself. Our hope is to plant the seed of sustainability in your head.

1.
Can we refuse flyers and free samples?

2.
Can we reduce our consumption of packaged
products and new clothes?

3.
Can we reuse our containers and
bags and buy in bulk?

4.
Can the container of the product we are
considering buying be recycled?

5.
Can we compost to enrich our soil?

# Incorporating simplicity into your daily life

Taking care of yourself doesn't have to be complicated or require complex rituals. We love taking a moment to pause by incorporating simple actions and low-cost activities into our daily lives. Here are some of our favourites.

### Go for a walk in nature

Did you know that the location of your walk has a direct effect on your physical and mental health? And that walking in a forest increases creativity and serenity, and strengthens the immune system?

We love going for hikes outside, even more so now that we have children. On weekends, or even during the week, we often set off for hiking adventures. There's no need to go far. There are several beautiful trails within an hour of where we live. Even if it's just a walk to a nearby park, whenever you head out, leave your cellphone at home so that you can be fully present. But what does being "fully present" mean? It means observing your surroundings: the trees, the flowers, the details. It means smelling the air, the different scents of foliage and blossoms and soil. It means hearing all the sounds: the birds, the wind in the leaves, even the cars or the people around you. In short, it means taking time to reconnect with nature so that you appreciate it more.

## Take a bath

It might seem trivial, but making the time to run yourself a bath with added essential oils (ylang-ylang, lavender, rosemary, bergamot, jasmine, and so on), lighting a few candles, putting on your favourite playlist, or escaping into the pages of a book can make a real difference in a stressful day or week.

If you wish, you can even turn the bath water into a mini spa by adding a small cotton bag of tea, dried flowers, or oats to infuse the water. This method softens the water (in the case of oats) or adds antioxidants (in the case of tea) that are good for the skin.

**RECIPE FOR A CALMING BATH SACHET**

In one sachet or small cloth bag, place:

3 tbsp (30 ml) dried lavender flowers

3 tbsp (30 ml) dried Roman chamomile flowers

1 cup (250 ml) oat flakes

Add the sachet to a hot bath and let it steep while you relax.

Compost your little mix after use, and wash and reuse the bag!

 Attention

Having a bath isn't necessarily the most eco-responsible option in terms of water consumption, so we make it into a special occasion and really enjoy it!

## Indulge in self-care treatments

We admit that this is a luxury. However, whenever our energy levels are low, we like to book some acupuncture, reflexology, or a massage. These moments of precious relaxation build up our immune systems and lower our stress levels, making us less susceptible to seasonal depression. Spending money on a treatment is thus a long-term investment in our health.

## Eat meals with friends

Cook, get together with friends, and have a good time! There's nothing complicated about it. Everyone can bring a dish to lighten the host's workload. Moreover, it has been proven that sharing simple moments with friends is excellent for our mental health. It is no accident that *Canada's Food Guide* recommends it.

### Stéphanie's tip

For a more healthful morning routine, unplug so you can connect with yourself. Too many of us reach for our phones as soon as we wake up in the morning. I used to be one of them! How can we live simply and fully if we constantly allow ourselves to be bombarded with ads and information as soon as we open our eyes?

Over a year ago, I resolved to change my morning habits and to get up a little earlier. Whether you have 5 minutes, 30 minutes, or even an hour to spare in the morning, the goal with this routine is to always begin your day with a light heart. Work, social media, and cellphones can all wait their turn. Of course, everyone's family life is different, but don't shortchange yourself by saying you don't have enough time. Just give it a try!

## Make your own products

It's so satisfying to make homemade products. Often you can make them with ingredients you already have in your kitchen. Simplifying your life will have an impact on every aspect of your daily routine, including your beauty regime. This translates into using fewer products, but choosing ones with multiple uses. Ignore the advertisements cosmetics companies put out, telling us we need one cream for our legs, one for our eyes, another for our hands, and so on (see Chapter 5).

## Cook more

It's no secret that we love cooking. We often spend our free time cooking our favourite meals and snacks (see Chapter 4 for recipe ideas).

**OTHER SUGGESTIONS**

· Meditate.

· Establish a regular movement practice, like yoga.

· Go to the library and read a book.

· Create your own spa experience at home.

· Make a vision board.

· Garden.

· Draw or paint or craft.

# Small acts, big impact

1.
Avoid driving your car.
Choose to walk, cycle, or use public
transport whenever possible.

2.
Pay attention to your energy usage. Turn
off the lights when you leave a room, dry
your clothes outside, and unplug your
devices when they aren't in use.

3.
Replace your old lightbulbs with
energy-efficient LED bulbs.

4.
Eat at home more; eat out less.
Bring your lunch to work.

5.
Try to positively influence the people
around you (at work and at home) to do
more for the environment.

6.
Choose activities that are more
environmentally friendly.

7.
Reduce your consumption of animal
products (meat, dairy, seafood).

8.
Make your own cleaning products with
environmentally friendly ingredients.

9.
Wash your clothes less often, and use
cold water when you do wash them.

10.
Bring reusable containers
when you go out.

11.
Put a "no flyers" note on your mailbox.

12.
Stay informed and read up on
environmental issues.

13.
Vote for political parties who focus
on the environment in their policies
and manifestos.

14.
Regularly declutter your inbox.
Cloud storage consumes a lot of energy
and contributes to pollution.

15.
Buy carbon-offsets when you fly to
reduce your personal carbon footprint.

16.
Buy local and organic products
whenever possible.

17.
Support businesses that care
about the environment.

18.
Use up your leftovers to avoid food waste.

19.
Buy second-hand items rather than
new whenever possible.

20.
Insulate and draftproof your doors and
windows in winter to prevent energy loss.

21.
Run the dishwasher only when it's full.

22.
Lower your thermostat a few
degrees to save on fuel.

23.
Take short showers rather than baths.

24.
Open the windows in your house to
freshen the air rather than using
perfumed air purifiers.

25.
Install a rain barrel for watering
your plants.

26.
Compost.

27.
Use washable rather than
disposable wipes.

28.
Plant a garden or decorate your balcony
with a few plants or flowers.

# Choosing simplicity during the holidays and other special occasions

When you start following a zero-waste lifestyle, certain seasons are trickier than others. We have to constantly reaffirm our choices during winter celebrations (and holidays in general) when we are all faced with overconsumption. While we must respect other people's lifestyles, we can still bring our values to our choices of presents, abundance, and waste. Don't preach: A positive message is always better received than a negative one. Be a source of inspiration for those around you, and they will naturally follow your lead.

1. Ask for experiences (lessons, treatments, dining out) rather than material possessions. Such things are bound to remain in your memory far longer than objects.

2. Ask your family to collectively give the children one present instead of multiple smaller presents. This way, the kids will learn to appreciate their gifts and cultivate gratitude.

3. During the holidays, decorate your house with objects from nature, such as pine branches or pine cones, or use fabric scraps to make bunting.

4. Offer homemade presents (cookies in a jar, body lotion, scented candles, for example). Many recipes are very simple to make, and we enjoy adapting them to each individual recipient.

5. Get out the board games! There's no need to buy anything: You can invent your own, and the internet is full of ideas for low-cost games.

6. Suggest making your next gathering a potluck. The guests each bring a dish of their choice, which will allow everyone to discover new flavours.

# Chapter 2

# FASHION
# &
# HOME

"THE FASHION INDUSTRY IS
THE WORLD'S SECOND-LARGEST
POLLUTER AND ONLY 10 PERCENT
OF THE CLOTHES PEOPLE DONATE
TO CHARITY OR THRIFT STORES
GET SOLD."

*The True Cost* documentary

# An eco-responsible wardrobe

The fashion industry's recent rapid growth has led to clothes production doubling every year since the 2000s. The world now generates about 80 billion new pieces of clothing annually, the majority of which are made in Asia. This is 400% more than the amount we generated just two decades ago![1] With the modernization and invention of synthetic fabrics made from polymers, the fashion industry has indisputably become one of the world's worst polluters. And that's without even taking into account the unsustainable and unjust working conditions in these textile factories. Today more than ever, how you dress is a way to show your respect for the environment, express yourself, and make wiser choices.

When we first met, Laurie and I used to shop a lot. Whenever we had some free time, we would go out shopping. Neither of us had huge wardrobes bursting with shoes and barely worn clothes, but we consumed more than we really needed, especially things that were fashionable or on trend.

Once we changed our lifestyles and became more environmentally friendly, our priorities inevitably shifted, too. We started to understand the harm the textile and clothing industries wreak on our planet. We strongly recommend that you watch the documentary *The True Cost* to get a better understanding of the ecological issues at stake in this industry.

---

1. *The True Cost*, written and directed by Andrew Morgan (2015).

# Choosing
# better clothing

### Organize your wardrobe

Since we don't have big closets to hide our clothes in, we decided to store them in sight, on a rail and hangers in our bedrooms. By doing this, we can always see what we have. Next, we organize our clothing by type (sweaters, jackets, pants, etc.) and by colour. This often simplifies our morning routines when we have no idea what to wear!

We keep smaller items (socks, underwear, tanks, T-shirts, etc.) in a small dresser. Pro tip: Recycle or repair your holey socks, or get rid of them, because worn-out clothes are a burden.

With the changing seasons, it is important to rotate your clothes. This also gives you a chance to sort and rearrange everything. We keep space in our wardrobes to store our seasonal clothes and then take them out again at the appropriate moment. Consider sorting through your clothing regularly.

NOTE : For more on tidying, we recommend Marie Kondo's books.

## Create a minimalist wardrobe

Now that you've made all this space, look at what you really need and not at what is in fashion before you hit the shops. Avoid overly conspicuous patterns that won't stand up to the test of time and choose clothes that are basics, neutrals, and multipurpose.

Start the process of simplifying your wardrobe by first making a list of your current needs as you inventory the clothes you have (the ones you wear regularly, the ones that could be repaired or altered, and so on).

To help you develop a minimalist wardrobe, here is our list of essentials. Don't worry if you don't reach this point on your first attempt; it's actually pretty difficult to live daily life with thirty items max.

- Comfortable jeans in a classic style
- Black jeans or pants
- A white or black T-shirt
  (opt for cotton or natural fibres)
- Leggings that work for everyday
  wear and sports
- A few sweaters or jackets in colours
  that go with everything
- Comfortable underwear that you like
- High-quality socks
- A classic dress that can be dressed up
  for special occasions
- Running shoes
- A pair of classic shoes you can wear with more
  than one outfit for various kinds of occasions
- Seasonal clothes

### WHAT IS A MINIMALIST STYLE?

To create a style that is both minimalist and individual, it's crucial to learn how to mix and match different pieces. Each item of clothing should be carefully chosen to make you look your best. Opt for neutral colours or ones that suit your complexion. Making these choices means you will always like the clothes in your wardrobe because they make you feel good — which also means you will take better care of them and they will last longer. This is minimalism in a nutshell.

## Make ecologically responsible purchases

Whenever we need a new item of clothing, we first try to find it used. If we can't, we source it from a company near us that produces clothes locally. This can sometimes be more expensive, but when it is a quality piece in a classic or minimalist style, you will keep it for longer.

One more thing: Only go shopping when you really need something. If you feel the need to go for a stroll around the mall, go for a hike instead.

## Opt for fabric made from natural fibres

Fabrics made from natural fibres are not only more resistant and durable, but they also reduce the ecological impact of our wardrobe. It has been shown that polyester, acrylic, and nylon, to name just a few, not only release toxins into the water when they are washed, but also often cause skin allergies. The best fibres to choose include wool, silk, linen, cotton, hemp, leather, and denim.

Choose high-quality, comfortable jeans. Several companies now sell jeans that are more environmentally responsible, made with organic fibres or plant-based dyes. It is not necessary to have three or four pairs in different styles or colours.

# Repair your clothes to give them a new lease on life

Before throwing away a piece of clothing, we try to see some new potential in it. Take your shoes to the cobbler to fix them up, and if you aren't able to repair your own clothes, see a tailor.

**GIVE YOUR**
**CLOTHING A SECOND LIFE**

· Cut off your jeans to make shorts.

· Use old sweaters (preferably cotton) to make wipes, makeup-remover pads, or rags.

· Make cushions with your old wool sweaters.

· Make holiday garlands out of old sweaters.

· Dye your faded clothes with natural products (see page 46).

Dye your worn-out clothes or sheets with natural dyes made from food.

· Turmeric for brilliant yellow
Bring a large pot of water to a boil. Add turmeric powder and stir until dissolved. Carefully submerge the fabric to be dyed. Let the water simmer over low heat for an hour. Turn the heat off and let the water cool. Rinse the dyed fabric under cold running water, and then machine wash.

· Black beans for powder blue
Soak dried black beans in a large pot of cold water for 24 hours. Strain the beans, pouring the soaking liquid into a clean bowl or pot. Carefully immerse the fabric to be dyed in the soaking liquid for 24 hours. Rinse the dyed fabric under cold running water, and then machine wash.

· Avocado pits for pale pink
Remove all the flesh from your avocado pits. Place the pits in a large pot of water. Heat over low heat for an hour. Carefully immerse the fabric to be dyed in the hot water. Let the water simmer over low heat for an hour. Turn the heat off and let the water cool. Rinse the dyed fabric under cold running water, and then machine wash.

· Hibiscus flowers for light red
In a large pot, combine hibiscus flowers and water. Bring to a boil, reduce the heat, and simmer for an hour. Carefully immerse the fabric to be dyed in the hot water. Simmer over low heat for another hour. Turn the heat off and let the water cool. Rinse the dyed fabric under cold running water, and then machine wash.

NOTES

• These dyes work better on natural fibres (wool, cotton, linen). Results will vary depending on the plants and materials used.

• As a general rule, use the same weight of plants as the weight of your material. For a deeper colour, add more; for a lighter colour, add less.

• These are simplified recipes. For more information on the full techniques and to find out more about natural dying, see Rebecca Desnos's book *Botanical Colour at Your Fingertips*.

# Declutter your space

We can't talk about simple living without talking about decluttering. Have you ever noticed how light you feel after cleaning? The more we move toward a simple life, the more we want to free ourselves of unnecessary material goods. Whether it's clothing, ornaments, or tools, it is important to be choosy about what you bring into your house.

For us, decluttering was a gradual process over time. Some people prefer to declutter all at once. However, we firmly believe that if something is to become a habit, it is better to take small steps and move at a pace that suits you. The main thing is to overcome the fear of getting rid of your possessions. Don't be surprised if purifying your space brings up some strong emotions.

Our environment is a mirror for our thoughts and feelings: When our houses are clean, we automatically feel lighter, and vice versa. Once we slowly started detaching from our possessions, we realized that a large number of items were just gathering dust, while we were keeping others for sentimental reasons or purely because we didn't know how to get rid of them. There were also items we were holding on to in the hopes that we would one day be able to use them again. Sound familiar?

## TIPS FOR DECLUTTERING YOUR SPACE

1. Sort

   Working one room at a time, get rid of objects and projects that are no longer useful to you or that you are keeping simply because someone gave them to you. When you take on a room, do it fully (even the bathroom drawer full of hair elastics and bobby pins, or the nightstand drawer that just accumulates random useless objects). Above all, don't start the project midweek or you are likely to lose all motivation before you finish.

2. Donate or sell

   Once you have sorted through a room, ask your friends and family if any of your items would delight someone else, or could have a second life elsewhere. You can also try selling items online or take them to a donation centre that specializes in that kind of object (appliances, clothes, furniture, etc.).

3. Reorganize

   Once you have sorted through your possessions and decided what to keep, reorganize your cupboards and closets. Find a system that suits you and get organized. Being organized has multiple advantages: You can be more efficient in the kitchen, see what's in your pantry in a single glance, choose your outfit more quickly in the morning, and so on. As for interior design, you will end up with a cleaner space, something that reflects your style, furnished with carefully selected items. Get into the habit of putting away everything you use each day so you no longer have to pick up after yourself.

4. Resist

   Once you have decluttered your space, try not to replace the items you discarded with new things. We are used to abundance: Seeing a nearly empty closet might be disconcerting to start with, but remind yourself that you don't need anything more. It is highly satisfying to appreciate everything you own and take care of it.

# Buying second-hand

You can find online groups for exchanging clothes, or visit local thrift stores. Hosting a clothes-swapping party is a great way to bring some variety to your wardrobe. Do something fun and useful: Spend an evening with your friends while helping each other out. The things you don't like any longer might make someone else happy.

For the home, there are tons of antique stores and online sellers where you can buy quality furniture, sometimes with way more character than stuff bought new. As well as the furniture being longer-lasting than that from big chains like Ikea, it is often more affordable. Whether you're looking on Kijiji or Facebook Marketplace, you're likely to find anything you want. From storage boxes to fridges to couches, you just need a little patience — and some imagination for certain items. We enjoy taking the time to find a used piece of furniture and giving it a new life with a spot of sanding or a lick of paint.

Stéphanie's tip

Be careful when buying used clothes or furniture: We shouldn't purchase more just because it's cheaper. I've made this mistake many times, and now I take my time choosing what I need. The ultimate goal here is to understand your consumption and to reduce what you buy so it doesn't end up in thrift stores or waste-sorting centres. Key words: Choose better, aim for quality, take your time. And don't be tempted by something just because it's cheap and in good shape.

# Decorating your home

For the home and decorating, we choose quality materials and second-hand pieces, or even make our own. Furniture and décor made of plastic or that is poor quality tends to break quickly and is harder to recycle or reuse. Do your research and think carefully!

**DECORATING YOUR SPACE SIMPLY**

· Go treasure-hunting in antique stores
Unearth items and give them a second life. Just be careful not to start accumulating things again and telling yourself you're upcycling!

· Choose long-lasting materials
Wood, fabric, and stainless-steel items can be kept for a long time and repaired as necessary.

· Leave empty spaces
Yes, you read that right! Just keep things minimalist.

· Display your good china
If you have beautiful hand-made ceramic items, display them! We use trays in our kitchens to store our dishes and pots.

· Keep the essentials in sight
And store things you don't use often in a cupboard.

· Let the light in
A sheer curtain allows daylight into your home.

## Give your furniture
## and your interior a new life

Having fewer items in our houses brings us contentment and also allows us to take better care of what we have. Second-hand items and even furniture need a bit of love: It is easy to transform them with a little time and creativity. These types of refurbishments make great outdoor projects for the summer.

**SIMPLE TIPS FOR**
**REVIVING YOUR FURNITURE**

· Clean
Sometimes, a good cleaning is all it takes to bring an old piece of furniture back to life. Use vinegar and a rag to scrub most surfaces clean (be sure to check what kind of wood or varnish it is first).

· Paint
It's easy to paint straight onto furniture, or to sand it before treating with a natural varnish. Go to your local hardware store for expert advice.

· Change the handles
Sometimes a set of new drawer handles is all you need.

· Give your furniture a new use
A small wooden crate can become a nightstand. Search "Ikea hacks" on Pinterest, and you'll find a ton of options and ideas for transforming and repurposing Ikea furniture and accessories.

Stéphanie's tip

For my baby's bedroom, I wanted to find a small dresser that could be used as a change table as well as for storing clothes. After several fruitless months of scouring the internet, I found *the* piece, except it was in sad need of a little TLC. I took one of the drawers to the hardware store so they could advise me on how to restore it to its former beauty. Time, a good clean, a natural plant-based varnish, and new handles: That was all it took to bring that piece of furniture back to life and display its charm in a child's bedroom.

## Green up your home

Several studies have shown that the most economical and effective way of purifying the air in our houses, and indoors in general, is to add a few plants. Acting as a natural filter, plants clean the air of toxic vapours and also help to reduce our stress levels. They are therefore our main source of decoration. We find that plants bring a great deal of life to a room.

Create your own little oasis in your home. If you don't have a green thumb, here are a few varieties of easy-care plants (read: basically unkillable).

· Succulents

· Palms

· Philodendrons

· Aloe vera (as a bonus, you can use the gel from its leaves as an after-sun lotion or a hydrating face mask)

· Sansevieria (also known as snake plant or mother-in-law's tongue)

· Spider plants

· Pothos (we think these are the easiest, and they grow incredibly quickly)

· Miniature schefflera

· Pilea (Chinese money plants)

· Ivies

Carefully follow the recommendations for each species with regard to watering and soil and light requirements. Pay attention to your plants. You will see if they aren't doing well in a particular environment. Sometimes just moving them to a new spot brings them back to full health.

You can also take cuttings from some species (pothos, spider plant, monstera, succulent, pilea) to repot and give as gifts to friends and family.

Once a month, give your plants (with the exception of cacti and succulents) a good drink by putting them in the bath and showering them in tepid water to give the roots a good watering. This also helps to dust off the leaves.

 Laurie's tip

Use old jars with the labels removed to make industrial-style vessels for your plants. Watch online tutorials to make your own plant holders with string or wool. Simple, effective, and very pretty!

# DIY at home

**GREEN WALL**

There's nothing better than having a few climbing plants to bring a wall to life. Some species, like pothos or ivy, love to climb, and will quickly attach themselves to whatever support you give them. Choose a sunny wall, and put up a few push-pins to guide the branches. Over time, the plants will grow and help you create your very own green space.

**SEEDS**

In the spring, we use old egg cartons to start our seeds indoors before transferring the seedlings into the garden at the appropriate time. Simply fill each cup with a little garden soil and plant a seed in each one. Plastic clamshell containers (like the ones Boston lettuces come in) also make excellent mini-greenhouses for microgreens. No need to buy a new one each year — just use what you already have on hand.

## GROW A BEAUTIFUL PLANT FROM A PINEAPPLE

You will need:

Planter

1 pineapple

Water

Soil

1. When you buy a whole pineapple, cut off the top leafy part (the crown). Reserve the pineapple for eating. Peel off several layers of leaves, leaving the base of the crown exposed (approximately the bottom 2 inches). The leaves should come out easily and reveal a few brown nubs (the roots will grow from these nubs). It's important to scrape off all the pineapple flesh so that the stem doesn't rot.

2. Next, place the stem in a jar full of water and set aside (changing the water every day) until the roots start to grow.

3. After two or three weeks, when the roots have grown a few inches, plant the stem in a pot of soil.

4. If you use a lot of love and patience, you might one day be able to see your plant grow its own little fruit.

## CANDLE

It's incredible how a simple candle can provide a little atmosphere to a room. And since candles are so easy to make, why miss out?

You will need:

Double boiler

Wax (soy or beeswax)

A wick with a wick pin

A container (you could reuse a Mason jar or an antique glass cup)

Hot glue or sticky tape

A pencil

OPTIONAL: essential oils

1. Place the wax in the top of a double boiler over low heat. Heat, stirring occasionally, until the wax is completely melted.

2. Secure the base of the wick pin at the bottom of the container using hot glue or a bit of sticky tape to hold the wick in place while you're pouring the wax.

3. When the wax is melted, remove the pan from the heat. Stir in 30 to 40 drops of the essential oils, if using. Pour the mixture into your container of choice.

4. Carefully coil the top of the wick around a pencil (secure with a bit of tape, if needed) and place the pencil horizontally across the container to hold the wick straight.

5. Let the wax harden completely.

## POT OR VASE WITH DRIED FLOWERS

We love decorating our homes with eucalyptus or other flowers we've dried ourselves. It's an easy, low-cost way to brighten things up. During the holidays, use pine, spruce, or holly branches from outside.

There's no need to go out and buy a vase — simply use an empty wine bottle or something similar. A very effective way to remove labels is by washing the glass in hot water and then rubbing off the residue with a little lemon essential oil.

1. Choose fresh local flowers that dry quickly (eucalyptus, gypsophila, lavender, rose, wheat, poppy, buttercups).

2. Arrange your flowers in a beautiful bouquet and then tie the stems together with string — just not too tightly.

3. Hang the bouquet upside down, away from bright light, to dry.

4. Once the flowers are completely dry, carefully separate and arrange your bouquet in your chosen container.

# When you make your next purchases

1.
Buy used.

2.
Rent clothes for special occasions.

3.
Borrow an item instead of buying it whenever possible, or perhaps buy it with a group of friends.

4.
Choose products made of sustainable materials (wood, stainless steel, linen, cotton, etc.).

5.
When buying new, choose local and long-lasting products.

6.
Always prioritize quality over quantity.

7.
Think before you buy.
Beware of online shopping!

8.
Whenever you feel like going shopping, choose to go for a walk or try another activity to shift your focus.

9.
Repair an object or piece of clothing rather than replacing it.

10.
Ask yourself whether you really need it.

*Chapter 3*

# CLEANING

"ZEN TEACHING SHOWS HOW WE CAN PURIFY OURSELVES THROUGH HOUSEWORK AND CLEANING. RETURNING AN OBJECT TO ITS PROPER PLACE, TIDYING A ROOM, AND CLOSING THE DOOR ON A SPOTLESS AND ORDERED SPACE SYMBOLIZE OUR ABILITY TO SET THE WORLD TO RIGHTS. CLEANING SWEEPS AWAY NON-ESSENTIAL ACCRETIONS TO REVEAL THE ESSENCE OF MANKIND AND NATURE."

Dominique Loreau,
*L'art de la simplicité*

# A healthy mind
# in a clean house

People always feel better in a clean space: We have more energy, our thoughts are clearer, and we can finally rest. In fact, the state of our homes is very often representative of our mental state. Therefore, we shouldn't see housekeeping as a thankless task to be completed every week, but rather as a ritual that cleanses our minds.

For us, cleaning means taking the time to look after our things, fuss over them a little, and notice them. And given that we love every item we have in our houses, we want to take care of them so they will last as long as possible. A minimalist home often requires less time to clean, because there aren't endless objects to dust or lots of furniture to move around and clean behind.

We also like to use natural products to clean our houses. We make most of these items ourselves, but you can buy environmentally friendly ones. Contemporary cleaning products give off volatile organic compounds, which we then breathe in, or they contain toxic ingredients that find their way into our water sources and eventually contaminate our bodies. So it's important to pay attention to what you use to clean your home and your clothes.

## Be aware of products claiming to be green

Some companies are taking advantage of the environmental movement to promote products they claim are green when they are really nothing of the sort. Read labels carefully so that you know you are choosing products made without toxic ingredients like fragrances, formaldehyde, benzene, methanol, ethylbenzene, and toluene.

Although household cleaners are regulated by Health Canada, certain substances are allergenic, irritating, or even carcinogenic when used for a long period of time. In addition, the danger increases if you combine several products. If you see the death skull on your cleaning bottles, it's best just to stay away.

Real life according to Laurie

Use up your products before starting to make your own or buying environmentally friendly ones. The environmental impact is the same as if you just threw everything out right away. If you really feel the need to get rid of products immediately, donate them to animal shelters or homeless shelters, which often accept cleaning supplies.

## Simple and effective cleaning

One single product is often enough to clean most surfaces. It's pointless having a whole range of various kinds of cleaners in your cupboard, one for each room in your house. We like multipurpose products made with safe, natural ingredients, and that are also good for keeping our environment healthy. By reducing the number of cleaning products in your house, you will gain more space in your cupboards.

Draw up a cleaning schedule you can stick to so that you don't feel overwhelmed by the number of tasks you have to do, and involve all the members of your family with age-appropriate tasks. (Small children often love cleaning windows. Even if they don't do a perfect job, it teaches them collaboration and participation.)

Procrastination is the enemy of cleaning. Make the time enjoyable by playing some music or listening to a podcast, and giving yourself targets. Do one room at a time so as not to burn out.

─☼─ Caution

Dishwashers are the main source of air pollution in the house. The very hot water and the chemicals in dish soap release several pollutants into the air. Use a chlorine- and phosphate-free dish soap, and open a window while the dishwasher is running to minimize any toxic emissions.

# Cleaning essentials

- Baking soda
  (scouring, deodorizing, cleaning, degreasing, softening)
- Household* or white vinegar
  (disinfecting, degreasing, descaling, deodorizing)
- Essential oils: lemon and tea tree
  (deodorizing, antibacterial)
- Marseille or Castile soap
  (cleaning)
- Coarse salt

**FOR LAUNDRY**

- Marseille soap
  (cleaning, stain removing)
- Sodium percarbonate
  (bleaching, stain removing, disinfecting)
- White vinegar
  (softening, bleaching, disinfecting, colour fixing)
- Ecological detergent
- Baking soda
  (softening, stain removing, etc.)

* Household vinegar has a higher concentration of acetic acid
(the cleaning agent) than white vinegar. Avoid using vinegar on marble
or cement, as it can cause these materials to disintegrate.

# Spring cleaning

**SURFACES**

Hard surfaces can be cleaned with the same all-purpose cleaner (see recipes on page 86). Use this daily for a clean space.

**CARPET**

To deodorize a carpet, combine 1 cup (250 ml) of baking soda with 10 drops of an essential oil of your choice. Sprinkle the mixture on the carpet. Let it rest for 1 hour before vacuuming.

**MIRRORS & WINDOWS**

Mix a little vinegar with hot water, and use a rag or newspaper to wipe clean. Sometimes we also add drops of lemon essential oil for a fresh scent. Avoid cleaning on sunny days to reduce spots.

**CURTAINS**

We take our curtains down to wash them and hang them back up while they're still damp to avoid creases. This also saves time in drying and ironing.

## FLOORS

First, we give the floors a thorough vacuuming, moving the furniture to get at all the dust that has accumulated over the winter. Then, using a good old mop, we wash the floors with the following mixture: 4 cups (1 L) of hot water, 1 tablespoon (15 ml) of Castile soap, and 10 drops of essential oil (tea tree, rosemary, lavender, etc.). Wring the mop out well so as not to damage the floors with water. If your floors are waxed, use cold water.

## WOODEN SURFACES

Sprinkle wooden surfaces (cutting boards, counter) with coarse salt and then rub with half a lemon (lemon cleans and disinfects). Next, give furniture a little TLC by wiping some olive oil over them with a rag. For more delicate types of wood, simply clean with a well-wrung-out cloth and a little bit of gentle soap.

## BEDDING

We wash everything — pillows, duvet, sheets — and we hang it all outside to dry as well. Adding a few drops of tea tree oil to the laundry water will kill off any lurking dust mites.

For brighter whites, use sodium percarbonate, which is a more ecologically sound alternative to bleach.

## SINK, BATH, & SHOWER

Make a paste by combining two parts baking soda and one part water, and then rub the paste onto the surface in question with a clean sponge or rag to remove dirt. Finish by polishing chrome with white vinegar for a high shine. You could also add a few drops of lemon essential oil to the vinegar for a fresh scent.

## FRESHENING THE AIR

Open the windows! If you have an essential-oil diffuser, you can enjoy experimenting with oils to freshen the air, or even make yourself an air-purifying spray (see recipe on page 92).

### DID YOU KNOW?

The air indoors is often more polluted than the air outdoors, because of the numerous chemical products and volatile organic compounds in our houses. Open your windows and doors every day for 15 minutes to allow air to circulate around your house. This will also help rid your house of undesirable odours.

If you suffer from allergies, air out the house in the morning rather than in the evening — there are fewer allergens in the air at this time of day.

Real life according to Laurie

If you don't have the time, or simply don't want to start making your own homemade products, you can bulk buy most of these products in zero-waste stores or bulk stores.

# A few tried-and-tested recipes

**MAGIC SCOURING PASTE**

You only need two ingredients to make this homemade scouring paste. It scrubs perfectly, and also deodorizes surfaces (stainless steel, wood, enamel, tile). You will conquer all sorts of stains! However, avoid using it on aluminum or waxed surfaces.

You will need:

2 tbsp (30 ml) baking soda

1 tbsp (15 ml) water

OPTIONAL: 1–2 drops of Castile soap or dish soap

In a bowl, mix together baking soda and water until it forms a thick paste.

NOTE : For an even tougher cleaning paste, replace some of the water with Castile soap or dish soap.

## TOILET CLEANER

This mixture will leave your toilet sparkling clean!

You will need:

½ cup (125 ml) baking soda

¼ cup (60 ml) Castile soap or dish soap

10 drops of tea tree oil

OPTIONAL: 1/2 cup (125 ml) white or household vinegar

1. If your toilet bowl has a lot of limescale, first pour some coarse salt into the toilet bowl and leave it to soak for a few hours before scrubbing the mixture with a brush.

2. Pour all of the ingredients into the toilet bowl and scour with a toilet brush or an old washing-up brush (even greener!).

3. To disinfect the toilet, pour ½ cup (125 ml) of white or household vinegar into the toilet bowl and let it sit for a few hours before flushing.

Laurie's tip

Some brands of essential oils sell large sizes of lower quality oils. Use them to make your cleaning products. There's no need to use your best oils to clean your surfaces; the cheaper ones will be just as effective at disinfecting and perfuming your space, and will be more economical.

## CITRUS-PEEL VINEGAR

Instead of throwing your citrus (orange, lemon, clementine, grapefruit) peels straight into the compost, use them to make a citrus-scented cleaning vinegar. It's an effective cleaner and smells delicious.

You will need:

4-cup (1-L) Mason jar with a lid

Citrus peel (enough to fill the jar)

White vinegar (5%)

1 cup (250 ml) water

1. Place the peel in the Mason jar and add white vinegar to fill the jar, leaving about 1 inch of headspace. Cover with the lid and leave the jar in a cupboard for 2 weeks to let the mixture steep.

2. Strain the mixture (discard the solids) and pour the vinegar into a glass spray bottle, diluting it with equal parts water (1 cup of vinegar to 1 cup of water). Seal with the cap and shake well.

3. Use the vinegar as an all-purpose cleaner.

## ALL-PURPOSE CLEANER (TWO WAYS)

Here are two all-purpose cleaners that you can make at home in just a few minutes. They are very economical, and safe for both you and the planet.

You will need:

**VERSION 1**

Glass spray bottle

1 tbsp (15 ml) Castile soap

1 cup (250 ml) water

20 drops of essential oils of your choice

**VERSION 2**

Glass spray bottle

½ cup (125 ml) white vinegar (or citrus vinegar, see page 85)

1 cup (250 ml) water

20 drops of essential oils of your choice

NOTE : Vinegar tends to decompose plastic, so a glass spray bottle is a better choice here.

Combine all of the ingredients in your spray bottle. Cover with the lid and shake well.

Laurie's tip

Opt for essential oils with antiseptic properties (lavender, tea tree, lemon, clove, citronella, eucalyptus, pine, etc.). These will naturally disinfect your home and perfume it at the same time.

# Perfuming your home naturally

Scents are directly connected to our emotions. Everyone loves a house that smells good. But don't use chemical perfume sprays or plug-ins. You can easily perfume your house with natural ingredients that are better for your health.

Before you perfume your house, however, make sure to purify the air and clean everything. Don't attempt to mask unpleasant odours with perfumes or fragrances.

## Flowers and natural elements

Nature provides an abundance of materials you can use to perfume your home. In winter, choose eucalyptus bouquets and pine branches to bring the scent of the forest into your home. Spring is lilac season. In summer you can grow lavender, and then dry it to make sachets for scenting your drawers and closets.

## Incense

Burning incense is another great way to get rid of odours and create a more spiritual atmosphere. You can find it in stick or resin form to be burned on charcoal tablets.

Be sure to choose natural incense. Most incense sold in big-box stores is made with synthetic perfumes and ingredients.

## Essential oil diffuser

We love diffusing essential oils all year round. The practice cleans the air and keeps microbes at bay as well as creating a relaxing, rejuvenating atmosphere. Diffusers allow you to perfume a room in a short period of time; depending on which oil you choose, they can also have health benefits.

There are several types of diffusers on the market. Just remember that essential oils are very powerful, and you should read up on them before using. Consult a certified aromatherapist for personalized advice.

☼ Caution

Do not diffuse oils in the presence of young children, pets, or pregnant women.

## Homemade scented spray

Commercial sprays bought in stores are often made with ingredients that might not be the best for your health. Most of them contain synthetic perfumes, which are endocrine disruptors, or carcinogenic volatile compounds that can cause allergies or asthma (perfumes, formaldehyde, butane, etc.). The good news is that it is very easy to make your own at home using just a few ingredients. These sprays allow you to adjust the fragrance according to your taste or the season, and they are a very economical way of creating your own atmosphere.

**HOMEMADE SPRAY**

You will need:

Glass or metal spray bottle

1 tbsp (15 ml) vodka

¾ cup (175 ml) water

20 to 30 drops of essential oils of your choice

Combine all of the ingredients in your spray bottle. Cover with the lid and shake well.

## A FEW SUGGESTIONS FOR COMBINING ESSENTIAL OILS

· Floral
Lavender, geranium, grapefruit

· Restorative
Mint, grapefruit

· Holiday atmosphere
Cinnamon*, pine, orange, clove

· Odour neutralizing
Tea tree, lavender, eucalyptus, mint

· Relaxation
Lavender, orange, chamomile

*Cinnamon essential oil should always be used in
very small quantities, as it can irritate the respiratory system.

# Laundry

The laundry room is a very straightforward place to simplify. We often have too many products for various uses and in different fragrances. It's important to remember that the skin absorbs everything we put on it, and this is just as true of chemical products in laundry detergent and softeners. Synthetic perfumes, preservatives, bleaching agents, and phosphates are all harmful to us (as allergens, endocrine disruptors, carcinogens, etc.) as well as the water supply (lakes become contaminated with blue algae, for instance) — and all of these things can be found in most commercial laundry soaps.

Here are some ways to make your laundry more environmentally friendly.

---

**THE MAGIC OF BAKING SODA**

To eliminate persistent odours (sweat, pets, etc.) on clothes, soak them in a bowl of water with a little baking soda. This will kill all of the bacteria causing the bad smell. You can sprinkle baking soda in your shoes, too.

Baking soda can also be used in small quantities in your laundry to soften hard water and make your detergent more effective. And it's a highly effective degreaser. Avoid using on silk or wool.

## Stain removal

More effective than any commercial product we have tried in the past, and far more economical, Marseille soap works miracles.

Simply soak the stain with water and rub it with Marseille soap, then watch it disappear. Beware of imitations: Real Marseille soap is made with olive oil, not palm oil (which is very harmful to the environment) like its imitators. Marseille soap also has many other uses. You can use it to make an all-purpose cleaner, wash your clothes, or even as a shower soap.

For bright whites, we also love sodium percarbonate. Soak your stained or discoloured fabrics in a bowl of hot water (add 1–2 tablespoons of sodium percarbonate for each litre of water) for 24 hours and then wash them as normal to make them whiter than white.

## Laundry soap

Choose a natural, perfume-free, hypoallergenic detergent. Bulk buying is your friend here.

Another option is using soap nuts. They are compostable and come from a natural resource (the soap, or red ash, tree). Simply place a few nuts into a small mesh bag and put them in the washing machine with your clothes. The soap nuts can be reused up to three times and won't damage your clothes.

## Fabric softener

We haven't used softener for several years, and our clothes are doing just fine (the towels are actually more absorbent). Of all the laundry products out there, softeners contain the most chemicals. If you want to soften your clothes naturally, replace the softener with white vinegar, adding it to the softener compartment.

## Linen water

When we use natural laundry detergents, which rarely contain synthetic perfumes, our clothes are often unperfumed. If you want your clothes to have a pleasant scent, there's a simple solution: Make your own linen water to spray on your clothes once they are dried.

### MAKE YOUR OWN LINEN WATER

You will need:

Glass spray bottle

Distilled or previously boiled water

1 tbsp (15 ml) vodka

20 drops of essential oil of your choice (such as lavender, eucalyptus, citronella, geranium, bergamot, etc.)

Pour all of the ingredients into your glass spray bottle and shake well. Shake before use.

NOTE : You can use linen water to perfume curtains, sheets, cushions, couches, and any other textiles in your home.

 Caution

Be sure not to use linen water on more delicate fabrics such as silk.

## Dryer balls

Dryer balls allow clothes to be perfumed naturally in the dryer when you add essential oils (2 to 3 drops maximum), as well as reducing the drying time required by creating movement (just as adding tennis balls does) and preventing clothes from creasing.

To be effective, you need at least three dryer balls. Reduce the drying time when you use the balls. This will avoid static building up in your clothes, which occurs when overheated fibres effectively become electrically charged. Clothes made from synthetic fibres also produce a lot of static: It is better to dry these items on a clotheshorse.

Dryer balls will last for about 2 years, depending on usage, and they can be composted at the end of their life span, since they are made entirely from wool.

### Laurie's tip

Wash your clothes only when they are truly dirty. We tend to wash our clothes too often, which wears them out more quickly and wastes a lot of water. You can simply hang them up for a while to freshen them up.

# Chapter 4

# FOOD

# Rethinking our eating habits

The quality of the food we consume has changed enormously with the growth of the food industry. It's time to stop putting our heads in the sand and underestimating the negative impact of industrial agriculture on communities and ecosystems.

If we decide to simplify our lives and live more in harmony with nature, we inevitably have to rethink both our pantry and our eating habits. We are often unaware of the environmental cost of our daily meals, but with a little education and awareness, we can find many ways to make positive changes that alter our relationship with the food we eat and the way we eat it.

In our case, a large part of our lifestyle change started in the kitchen, growing out of our desire to reduce our consumption of packaged and processed products. It was a very simple change, but one that has allowed us to be in better health and to diversify what we eat. We also avoid all preservatives and other additives with unpronounceable names, and choose instead to enjoy cooking.

For example, when we take the time to cook, we get to know the ingredients we consume better while also reducing our purchases of packaged products. Some people might think that this new habit is very time consuming, but the opposite is true: If you cook in an organized way, it is quite effective and pleasant. Cooking double the amount and freezing the extra means that on those days when you are pressed for time there is always a ready-made meal on hand.

In this section, you will find countless tips for developing healthier and more environmentally friendly eating habits. Among other things, we will show you ways to be more effective when you cook and shop, and we will suggest zero-waste recipes and tips.

# Making better food choices

## In season and local

Buying food that is in season and local is ideal: It supports the regional economy as well as smaller-scale agriculture, while at the same time giving you healthier food. Local fruits and vegetables are also tastier and fresher, since they were picked when they were ripe. Although we are big fans of locavorism, given the reality of our environment and our geographical surroundings, we need to be flexible. In the summer it's easy to eat local fruit and vegetables, because they are plentiful and the market stalls are overflowing with local produce. But in the winter it's a different story altogether. From the moment the first frost hits, we have to adapt our consumption or find ways of preserving food so we can enjoy it in the colder seasons.

 Real life according to Stéphanie

I love tropical fruits, even though they aren't local. I love to eat pineapples, lemons, oranges, and a lot of bananas. So I choose organic varieties because these foods are also very healthy.

## Support organic farms

Supporting small local farms changes our relationship with food, creating trust between us and our favourite growers, and helping those whose mission it is to farm more intelligently and eco-responsibly. We prefer certified organic produce to reduce our exposure to pesticides and to give this agricultural model a little help. This also allows us to use our fruits and vegetables without peeling them, because we don't have to worry about the chemicals their skins might have absorbed. This reduces prep time.

Joining a community-shared agriculture (CSA) scheme or shopping at your nearest farmers' market are two great options that will inspire you to eat local. These alternatives to conventional supermarkets offer products with superior freshness — often they have travelled just a few kilometres to reach our plates. Look up "family farmers network" if you live in Quebec or some parts of New Brunswick and Ontario, or just search online for a local CSA.

## Meet the farmers

Pick-your-own and agritourism allow you to visit producers while acquiring fresh, sun-kissed produce. Give it a try and see how much better the fruits and vegetables seem to taste when you've picked them yourself. Every year during berry and apple seasons, we go and pick huge quantities to stock up for winter. Find out about the different kinds of pick-your-own available near you.

### Laurie's tip

We regularly visit sellers to ask for their ugly fruit ("imperfect" fruit that is deemed unacceptable for the shelves but is perfectly fine for consumption). Ugly fruit is often cheaper, and still very beautiful! We use it to make jam, compotes, and smoothies.

People sometimes think local fruit and vegetables are boring, but you can find a multitude of recipes to prepare them in many different ways.

## SOME WAYS TO PRESERVE FRUIT AND VEGETABLES FOR WINTER

- Freezing

  (Best for strawberries, raspberries, blueberries.) Wash the fruit well and slice, if needed. Spread the fruit in a single layer on a baking sheet lined with reusable parchment paper, and place the pan in the freezer for 1 hour or until the fruit is frozen solid. Store in a reusable freezer bag or a glass container.

- Jam-making

  (Chia seed jam!) We love making large quantities of chia seed jam with our soft fruits. We freeze it in small Mason jars so we have a supply all year round.

- Pickling

  Cabbage, carrots, and cucumbers are all excellent candidates for home pickling.

- Coulis

  Collect your imperfect fruit in a container in the freezer. When the container is full, empty the contents into a large pot with a little water, some lemon juice, sugar, and vanilla or cinnamon. Cook until the fruit is very soft. Using an immersion blender, purée until smooth. Continue cooking until the mixture is reduced to the consistency of coulis. Strain through a fine-mesh sieve, using the back of a wooden spoon to push through the solids. Refrigerate for up to a week or freeze for up to 4 months.

- Compote

  We are crazy about apple compote made with apples from our favourite organic orchard. Because it's an organic farm, we can even keep the peel on when we make our compote. We also love using apple compote in our recipes in place of oil or fat.

# Become vegetarian(ish)

The global demand for meat has doubled since the 1950s. Unfortunately, this increased carnivorous appetite has an enormous environmental footprint. Intensive meat-raising is one of the most polluting industries on the planet. Deforestation, increased methane production, antibiotic overuse, and the mistreatment of animals should be the concerns that come to mind whenever you grill a steak on the barbecue.

Even if you aren't ready to become fully vegetarian, reducing the amount of meat you eat on a daily basis is a good start. Eating less meat is not only good for the planet, but it also reduces the risk of cardiovascular and inflammatory diseases. If you are a big meat eater, we suggest you try meatless Mondays — and for the rest of the week make an effort to buy healthier organic and antibiotic-free meats.

A whole range of plant-based proteins are now available that will provide you with a more balanced, lower-fat diet. We often think of tofu and pulses, but some fruits, vegetables, and whole grains also contain proteins, so it's easy to switch out the meat in many recipes.

- Shepherd's pie
  Replace the meat with lentils or textured vegetable protein (TVP).
  Sold in bulk stores, this kind of tofu can be quickly rehydrated in
  water. It also absorbs the flavours of the spices and stock it is
  cooked in. It is an excellent substitute for ground beef.

- Burgers
  You can find many recipes for homemade vegetarian patties online.
  Choose one based on black beans, kidney beans, or tofu.

- Fajitas or tacos
  Cubed cooked sweet potatoes, peppers, and kale make a great filling
  for homemade fajitas or tacos. We dress ours with our favourite
  cashew cheese recipe. Nom nom! (See recipe on page 143.)

- Sandwiches
  Build your veggie sandwich on a base of homemade hummus, a
  tofu spread, or a rustic lentil pâté.

- Asian-inspired stir-fry
  Choose edamame, tempeh, cubes of marinated tofu, or simply
  vegetables, cashew nuts, or a peanut-based sauce.

Stéphanie's tip

Having been vegetarian for more than 8 years, I found it was no big stretch to
cut out dairy products, too. My secret for adding the flavour of cheese without the dairy is nutritional yeast. I am completely hooked on the stuff. I sprinkle
it on popcorn and salad, and use it in my vegan cheese recipes. What's more,
it's bursting with vitamin B12, which is a vital supplement for vegetarians
because it is mostly found in animal products.

# Buying in bulk
# or packaging-free

A quick look at any grocery store shows the incredible amount of plastic packaging on the market. Plastic harms the environment and pollutes water. Every minute, the equivalent of one garbage truck filled with plastic is poured into the oceans.[1] And in Canada, 3 million tons of plastic waste are produced every year, while only 10 to 12% of this waste is recycled.[2]

What's more, we pay for this packaging that we could manage perfectly well without. Take a banana, for example: It will stay just as fresh if it is not placed in a plastic bag, because nature, which does all things well, has given it its own natural protection, otherwise known as its peel, which we remove before eating. So whenever possible, choose foods without packaging. It is often said that we vote with our money, so the next time you go to the grocery store, choose bulk foods rather than those packed in Styrofoam. Small choices like this will move our supermarkets in a green direction.

1. http://www3.weforum.org/docs/WEF_The_New_Plastics_Economy.pdf
2. https://www.canada.ca/en/environment-climate-change/services/managing
-reducing-waste/zero-plastic-waste/canada-action.html

Did you know that the largest proportion of waste in residential garbage is usually food packaging? We encourage you to let your grocery store know about your desire for change, because the more people who request fresh produce without packaging, the more we will reduce the quantity of plastic in the environment.

The number of bulk and zero-waste businesses is increasing every year, which is excellent news for the environment. Simply bring your reusable containers and bags when you go shopping, and fill them with the amount you need. As well as promoting a decrease in our plastic dependency, these actions allow you to buy food in smaller quantities, which considerably reduces food waste. Nowadays you can find everything in these stores, from toothpaste to animal food to laundry soap.

The good news is that many of the big chains are moving toward allowing consumers to bring reusable containers to the butcher, deli, and fish counters to reduce overpackaging. Stay informed.

Real life according to Stéphanie

Even though we buy almost all our groceries packaging-free, sometimes we make exceptions and buy packaged products. Yes, even we sometimes like to eat chips or buy a can of chickpeas just in case. We believe it's essential to give yourself a little latitude when it comes to both the unexpected and guilty pleasures.

# Organizing your pantry

Knowing how to manage and store your foods helps you avoid waste. Before reorganizing, you will need to declutter. Open up your drawers and cupboards, and work out what you have. Keep the stuff you use daily and give away or sell what you can do without. You will gain more storage space and can take an exact inventory of your possessions. It's easy to forget those little treasures hiding at the back of the cupboard!

Here are our organizational tips for a more functional kitchen.

**IS IT MORE EXPENSIVE TO BUY IN BULK?**

Since we like to buy organic, it is possible that buying in bulk might be more expensive. However, this choice is a no-brainer if you take into account the positive effects on the environment and our health. In our budgets, we prefer to allocate more to groceries and save elsewhere; in particular, spending less on clothes, accessories, prepared meals, trips, etc. We should, however, point out that some of the products we use on a daily basis are better value at big-box stores. We also buy certain products by the kilogram through a bulk-purchasing group that has several pick-up points in Quebec. By shopping in bulk, we have access to a wide range of products, and we can buy in smaller quantities to avoid food waste. One great advantage of bulk shopping: No need to buy a big bag of sorghum flour (for instance) for a recipe that only needs a small amount.

## Store your food in glass jars

When we began to be interested in the zero-waste movement, we immediately acquired some high-quality glass jars (Ikea's recycled glass jars are very practical) to store our dry food in and to help us organize our pantries. We encourage you to ask your grandparents for their old Mason jars and to shop at antique stores, because reusing is always better for the environment.

Nowadays, we buy nearly all our foods in bulk in our own jars, or we take reusable bulk bags because jars can be heavy to carry.

Cooking also becomes so easy and fast. No more flour bags that open themselves or foods that get damp. Open the jar and close it again — no waste!

 Stéphanie's tip

Reuse your commercial jars from sauce, salsa, mayonnaise, etc.
A pointer for removing the labels from your jars: Soak the jar
in hot water, remove the label, and rub the sticky residue with
a soft cloth and a few drops of lemon essential oil.

**GLASS JARS HAVE SEVERAL ADVANTAGES**

- Easy to organize and see what's inside
- Easy to wash
- Don't retain odours
- Attractive
- Very long-lasting (which is why there are so many in vintage stores)
- Multi-use (smoothies, salads, soup, flour, etc.)

## Label the jars

Since we don't have cupboards full of cookies, commercial cereals, or other packaged snacks, all our storage space is dedicated to our jars.

It is important to label them well so that you can find things easily, and so that all members of the family know what they contain.

**LABELLING**

· We love the famous DYMO labelling machine with its cute vintage style. You can find used ones, and we recommend sharing it between a group of friends. We stick these labels on the jars of the foods we eat regularly (quinoa, rice, flour, etc.) so that we don't have to constantly make new labels.

· For jars whose contents change more frequently, we use an oil- or water-based Sharpie marker: The ink can be erased easily, and the marker is also useful for labelling lunches and snacks.

## Rotate your foods

We frequently cook with the same basic ingredients (flour, rice, pulses, etc.), but to ensure a diversity of foods in our diet, especially when there is limited storage space, we like to rotate things. Among other advantages, this helps us switch things up and try different flours or pulses, and avoids having foods spoil at the back of the cupboard.

When buying in bulk, we can access a great diversity of products, which means we can buy in smaller quantities and avoid waste. So we rotate our staples: One week we cook with chickpeas, the next with black beans; one week with spelt flour followed by a sorghum flour week; one week penne, the next spaghetti; and so on.

As for the ingredients we use every day (rice or flour), we find it to be more economical to buy large quantities. We keep a small amount in a jar and store the rest.

Stéphanie's tip

Buy dried pulses and cook them in large batches. Freeze what you don't need right away in glass containers. Glass jars are economical and, more importantly, reduce the use of excess packaging.

# Reducing
# kitchen waste

Most of the trash we produce comes from the kitchen. Pay attention to the things you throw away most often (snack packets, paper towels, food containers). Start by reducing the non-essentials, or things that can be replaced by reusable products. Deep down, do we really need super-absorbent paper towels?

Don't go out and buy everything all at once; start by replacing a few items at a time. You can also make your own.

- Reusable dish towels or paper towels (such as Kliin)
When you decide to remove paper towels from your kitchen, you will realize how easy it is to manage without them and use a cloth instead.

- Reusable snack bags
One of the biggest sources of waste is often found in lunchboxes: the ubiquitous zip-top bag. More and more companies are offering attractive reusable snack bags for the whole family. There is an initial investment, but they will last for several years.

- Beeswax wrap
Replace single-use plastic wrap with sheets of reusable and compostable beeswax wrap (such as Abeego). In addition to being an ideal solution for reducing plastic use, these wrap sheets help to keep food fresh. Simply wash them by hand in cold water and they will last between 1 and 2 years.

- Silicone baking mats
Silicone is the perfect replacement for wax and parchment paper. Not only is it ultra-durable, it's also non-stick, so you don't have to grease the tray. This is a true kitchen essential.

- Reusable bags
This classic needs no introduction. Keep them near your front door or in your purse so you always have them ready to go. Reusable bags made from natural fibres are much more washable, which solves the hygiene problem of grocery bags, and are far more attractive. To compensate for the carbon footprint of the cotton production in this kind of bag, you need to keep reusing them, but this is in keeping with the minimalist lifestyle. Own fewer things and take care of them: If your cotton bag rips, you can repair it instead of throwing it away.

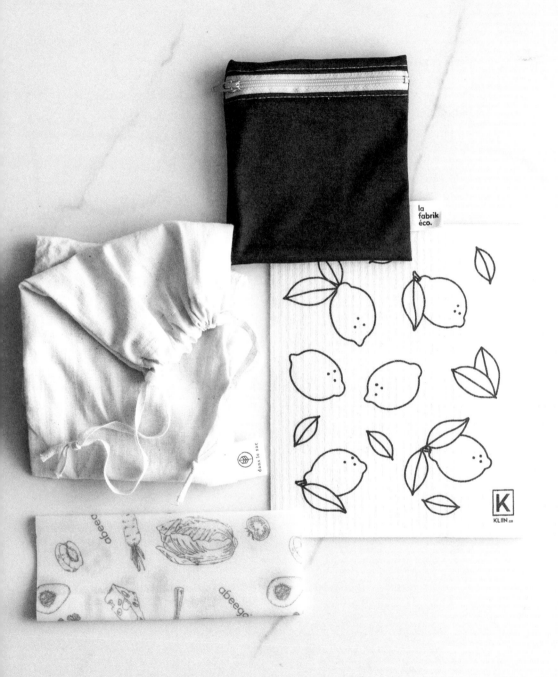

## Kitchen equipment

Have you noticed how all kinds of gadgets and duplicate utensils can accumulate in kitchen drawers and cupboards? Do we really need two peelers, three spatulas, two whisks, one pizza wheel, and so on?

**OUR ESSENTIAL KITCHEN TOOLS**

- A high-quality mixer
- One or two good knives
- A bread knife
- A wooden spoon and a wooden spatula
- A stainless-steel ladle
- A wide silicone spatula
- Measuring spoons and cups
- A digital scale
- A wooden chopping board
- Pyrex mixing bowls (two different sizes)
- A strainer
- Good-quality pots (three different sizes)
- A cast-iron frying pan
- A non-stick frying pan
- Pyrex oven dishes (two sizes)
- A bread pan or muffin pan
- A baking sheet
- An electric whisk (not an essential, but something we often use when making cosmetics)
- A peeler
- A microplane grater

# Preparing your bulk-shopping supplies

For many people, "zero waste" means going to the grocery store with reusable bags. And it's true that a significant proportion of our waste comes from packaging and from the products available at the grocery store, but it's also a result of our overconsumption, since we often buy more than we need.

We know that going bulk shopping for the first time can be intimidating, so we have prepared some tips and a list of necessary equipment to help you.

## Use a list to plan out your purchases

When you start bulk shopping, it's easy to spend hours looking at all the products and being overwhelmed by the variety. If you want to be efficient — and show up with enough storage containers — come armed with a list (especially if you don't live near the store).

Take a look through your cupboards to see what is running low or decide what you would like to try out this week. Then write down everything you need so you can be sure to bring enough containers (see next page).

## Use containers for liquids (glass or plastic)

Once you've written your list, choose which containers to bring. We bring glass containers for liquids (oils, vinegars, sauces), household products, and spices.

## Choose reusable bags for bulk dry goods or fruits and vegetables

For all dry goods, we use bulk bags made from washable material. They can even be used for flour or ground coffee. Check your list, and then bring a few extras for last-minute purchases. We also use these bags for fruits and vegetables, although most of the time we let our produce roam free in the cart.

## Take reusable bags for carrying your purchases

Now you have to transport all these fine purchases home. Remember to bring a reusable bag, a basket, or a backpack because bulk items can be very heavy and cumbersome. We like to keep a bag near the front door or in the car so it's always on hand.

## Choose where to shop

More and more zero-waste grocery stores are popping up in Canada. This means we don't have to travel too far to stock up.

Stéphanie's tip

In some areas it can be difficult to find bulk-shopping stores. In this case, it might work better to buy larger quantities in big-box stores and divide items up among friends and family. This can be a considerable reduction in cost and packaging. We've said it before and we'll say it again: Every action counts.

# Four zero-waste cooking ideas

## Homemade stock from vegetable peelings

We save our vegetable peelings and chicken bones in a sealed container in the freezer. When we feel like making a tasty soup, we take out the scraps and put them in a big stockpot with herbs, spices, and a few root vegetables (carrots, onions, garlic). Then we cover it with water, let it simmer for 2 or 3 hours, and bingo! Homemade stock for all those recipes that need a little lift, or for drinking when you're suffering from a cold.

The vegetable scraps can finish their life in the compost with the knowledge that they have done everything they could with their lives.

## Apple compote with peel

Every year we visit the same organic orchard. We buy a crate of "ugly" apples that can't be sold to stores but that make excellent compote. We leave the skin on to avoid waste, which results in a pretty pink colour.

 Laurie's tip

Do you have several bits of leftovers that need eating up? Be creative and improvise a tapas evening. Enjoy all those small plates while emptying out your fridge. This will save you from having to throw out food.

### Never throw away stale bread again

All good things must come to an end, and sometimes bread goes stale before you can eat it all. But this is no reason to throw it in the garbage.

Use up several-day-old bread by toasting it for a few minutes in the oven, letting it cool, and then turning it into homemade breadcrumbs in the food processor.

You can also cut toasted day-old bread into small pieces, spread them out on a baking sheet, and drizzle with olive oil, salt, pepper, and garlic to produce lovely homemade croutons for salads and soups.

For those who have a sweet tooth, use up stale bread by making a bread pudding or French toast.

### Smoothie popsicles

Made too much smoothie for breakfast? Pour the leftover mixture into popsicle moulds for healthy iced treats.

**STORING FRESH HERBS**

Store fresh herbs, spring onions, and lettuces upright in a jar or container with a little water (like flowers in a vase) in the fridge. Cover the roots with water and your herbs and veggies will stay beautiful for longer.

# Our favourite recipes

Although cans are recyclable (even so, more than 80 billion new cans are produced globally each year), we like to buy our pulses dried. It is not only more economical but also better for your health — cans often contain BPA (bisphenol A) and other chemicals. Once a week, we soak and cook a batch of pulses so we can incorporate them into our meals and make delicious recipes like this homemade hummus — which just happens to go perfectly with our homemade crackers (page 149).

Makes about 4 servings

You will need:

2 cups (500 ml) cooked chickpeas

3 tbsp (45 ml) tahini

1 garlic clove, roughly chopped

1 tsp (5 ml) garam masala or ground cumin + extra for garnish

1 tsp (5 ml) chili powder

2 tbsp (30 ml) olive oil + 2 tbsp (30 ml) for garnish

⅓ cup (85 ml) water

Juice of half a lemon, or more to taste

Salt and pepper to taste

1. Put the cooked chickpeas in a blender.

2. Add the tahini, chopped garlic, spices, 2 tbsp (30 ml) olive oil, water, lemon juice, and salt and pepper.

3. Cover with the lid and blend until smooth.

4. Transfer the hummus to a serving dish. Garnish with a drizzle of olive oil and a pinch of garam masala or cumin.

## HOMEMADE NUT MILK

Nut milk is an excellent source of protein, and this recipe can be adapted to your taste. Making your own milk at home allows you to control the ingredients and means you know it contains no additives. And it tastes way better!

Makes about 4 servings

You will need:

1 cup (250 ml) almonds

3 cups (750 ml) water
(ideally filtered)

Pinch of salt (optional)

1 tbsp (15 ml) pure maple syrup
(optional)

1 tbsp (15 ml) pure vanilla extract
(optional)

1. Soak the almonds in a bowl of cool water for at least 8 hours. It's easiest to soak them overnight and make your milk in the morning.

2. Strain the almonds in a colander and rinse under cool running water. Transfer the rinsed almonds to a food processor. Add the 3 cups (750 ml) water and the salt, maple syrup, and vanilla, if using. If you want to give your almond milk a particular flavour, this is the time to get creative.

3. Cover with the lid and blend on high speed for 2 minutes.

4. Pour the mixture through a nut-milk bag or a cloth bulk bag and into a bowl to filter it. The aim is to separate the almond pulp from the milk.

5. Reserve the pulp to add to other recipes (muffins, crepes, granola, crackers, etc.).

6. Pour your almond milk into your favourite container and refrigerate until ready to use.

NOTE : The milk will keep for 3 to 5 days in the fridge. You can also freeze a portion to make it last longer, but this could give the milk a yellowish colour.

## CASHEW NUT CHEESE WITH HERBS

We love this recipe, which makes a great substitute for traditional cream cheese. It's very easy to make, and everyone loves it, even people who love real cheese.

Makes about 6–8 servings

You will need:

1 cup (250 ml) raw cashew nuts

2–3 tbsp (45 ml) flaked nutritional yeast

2 tbsp (30 ml) fresh lemon juice

2 tbsp (30 ml) water (add more if you'd like a spreadable cheese)

1 tsp (5 ml) apple cider vinegar

1 clove garlic

½ tsp (2.5 ml) sea salt

Ground black pepper to taste

Finely chopped fresh herbs to taste (basil, oregano, thyme, chives, etc.)

1. Soak the cashew nuts in a bowl of hot water for 30 minutes (or in cool water overnight), then drain.

2. In a high-speed blender or the bowl of a food processor, combine the soaked nuts, nutritional yeast, lemon juice, water, vinegar, garlic, and salt and pepper. Blend until very smooth and creamy, 2 to 3 minutes.

3. Line a bowl with cheesecloth, letting the excess cloth overhang the edge of the bowl. Pour the cashew cream into the bowl. Wrap the mixture in the cheesecloth and squeeze tightly to remove excess liquid.

4. Place the wrapped mixture back in the bowl and refrigerate overnight. The cheese will gradually harden.

5. Unwrap the chilled cheese and coat with the finely chopped herbs. Serve with fresh bread, crackers, and grapes.

NOTE: Sometimes we can't wait until the morning to eat it. For a simpler version, you can also transfer the cheese directly to a small container, to keep it packed together, instead of placing it in a cheesecloth.

Will keep in the fridge in an airtight container for up to 5 days.

*Recipe adapted from Prana Biovegan Inc.*

We love making homemade snacks. These date energy bites are the perfect antidote for afternoon slumps. We double the recipe and put some in the freezer. This means there's always a little something on hand for road trips or cravings.

You will need:

1 cup (250 ml) pitted dates

¼ cup (60 ml) nut butter (almond, hazelnut, or peanut)

½ cup (125 ml) almonds or nuts of your choice

¼ cup (60 ml) oat flakes

3 tbsp (45 ml) unsweetened cocoa powder

Combine all of the ingredients in a food processor and mix until well combined. Shape the mixture by hand into small balls. Store the energy bites in an airtight container in the fridge or freezer.

## BREAKFAST SMOOTHIE BOWL
## WITH LOCAL BERRIES

This recipe will get your day off to a good start. We love smoothies, but we also enjoy taking the time to sit down and "eat" a smoothie with a spoon for breakfast. It's like eating ice cream first thing in the morning!

This super-healthy and vitamin-packed recipe is easy to adapt. Use whatever you have and garnish your smoothie bowl however you like.

You will need:

¼ cup (60 ml) nut milk (more or less, depending on desired consistency; see recipe on page 140)

1 banana

½ cup (125 ml) frozen blueberries

TOPPINGS: chia seeds, granola, nut butter (almond, peanut, or other), fruit (banana, strawberries, or other)

1. Place all the ingredients in a blender, cover with the lid, and blend until it reaches your desired consistency.

2. Transfer the mixture to a bowl and garnish with your desired toppings.

NOTE: We use frozen fruit because it yields a thicker, more consistent texture. We buy several bananas and let them ripen on the counter. Once they are quite brown, we remove the peel and freeze the banana so we always have some on hand. And frozen bananas make the best smoothie bowls.

## GRANOLA

Whether you enjoy it as is, use it as a smoothie topping, or eat it like cereal with nut milk, granola is simple and quick to make at home.

This is our version, but feel free to modify the ingredients and quantities according to taste and whatever is in your cupboard.

You will need:

3 cups (750 ml) oat flakes

½ cup (125 ml) seeds (sunflower, pumpkin, etc.)

½ cup (125 ml) coarsely chopped nuts (almonds, pecans, hazelnuts, etc.)

¼ cup (60 ml) melted coconut oil

¼ cup (60 ml) pure maple syrup

¼ tsp (1 ml) salt

OPTIONAL: chia seeds, flaxseeds, buckwheat, dried fruit, etc.

1. Preheat the oven to 350°F (180°C). Line a baking sheet with a silicone mat.

2. Place all of the ingredients in a large bowl and stir well.

3. Spread the mixture evenly over the prepared baking sheet.

4. Bake in the preheated oven for 30 to 40 minutes, stirring regularly with a spoon.

5. Remove the pan from the oven and let the granola cool completely. Store in an airtight container for several weeks.

## HOMEMADE CRACKERS

Cookies and crackers account for a large amount of the packaging in our cupboards. It's pretty hard to find packaging-free crackers, so we make our own. It's very easy, and lets us snack without the guilt.

You will need:

2 tsp (10 ml) sesame seeds

2 tsp (10 ml) chia seeds

2 tsp (10 ml) flaxseeds

½ cup (125 ml) unbleached all-purpose flour or spelt flour

½ cup (125 ml) whole-wheat flour

¼ tsp (1 ml) baking powder

¼ tsp (1 ml) salt

¼ tsp (1 ml) onion powder

¼ tsp (1 ml) garlic powder

¼ tsp (1 ml) ground turmeric

¼ cup (60 ml) water

2 tbsp (30 ml) olive oil

1 tsp (5 ml) liquid honey

1 egg yolk or a little milk for brushing

1. Preheat the oven to 325°F (165°C). Line a baking sheet with a silicone mat.

2. Combine the seeds in a bowl and set aside.

3. In another bowl, combine the flours, baking powder, salt, and spices. Add the water, oil, and honey. Stir until the mixture forms a dough.

4. On a floured work surface, knead the dough for about a minute, or until very smooth. Divide the dough into four equal balls. Using a rolling pin (or wine bottle), flatten each ball as thinly as possible and shape into a rectangle. Transfer the rectangles to the prepared baking sheet.

5. Using a pastry brush, paint the top of each rectangle with the egg yolk or milk. Sprinkle each piece of dough with the seed mixture, pressing the seeds down lightly so they stick to the dough.

6. Bake in the preheated oven for 16 to 18 minutes, or until the crackers are golden brown and crispy. Remove the pan from the oven and let the crackers cool completely.

7. Roughly break the cooled crackers into smaller pieces by hand. Store in an airtight container for up to a week. You can also freeze the dough to make the crackers later.

## PEANUT BUTTER AND CHOCOLATE DATES

Our favourite recipe for anyone with a sweet tooth. These bites are so tasty you forget that they are also good for your health ... in moderation, of course!

Makes about 8 servings

You will need:

1¾ cups (425 ml) chocolate chips

16 pitted dates

Nut butter (peanut or almond)

16 whole shelled peanuts or almonds

Fleur de sel

1. Line a baking sheet with a silicone mat.

2. Melt the chocolate in a double boiler over low heat.

3. Slice open the dates to create a pocket in each.

4. Spoon a small amount of nut butter into the middle of each date.

5. Place a peanut or almond on top of the nut butter.

6. Dip each date in the melted chocolate until completely covered and then place on the prepared baking sheet.

7. Sprinkle the chocolate-coated dates with fleur de sel.

8. Place the baking sheet in the refrigerator and chill until the chocolate hardens.

9. Transfer the peanut butter and chocolate dates to an airtight container. Store in the fridge for a few days, or in the freezer for up to a month.

# Gardening

For us, growing vegetables is a way to reconnect with nature and our food. In a fast-paced world, we love spending time cooking meals with fresh ingredients. And what could be fresher than something grown in your own garden?

It doesn't matter how much space you have, it's always possible to grow a few plants to liven up your meals. Basil and cherry tomatoes are perennial classics because they are easy to grow and don't need much space.

After a number of years, our gardening knowledge has improved, and although we still aren't perfect, we view the whole thing as a learning process. If a plant doesn't grow — or if we get an excellent harvest — we try to figure out why. We now know that several plants produce better when they are grown together. (The opposite is also true: Some plants harm each other, such as tomatoes and potatoes.) The technique of companion planting limits the use of pesticides and relies on biodiversity. It enriches the soil and repels insects. For example, when basil is planted near tomatoes it helps tomatoes produce more fruit, keeps away harmful insects, and improves the flavour of the tomatoes.

At the end of the season, harvest all of your herbs so you can dry them and use them in your meals year round.

Most importantly, don't forget to include plants and flowers that attract pollinating insects. As a result of pesticide use, bees and butterflies are becoming rarer in our gardens, but they are essential for our plants to produce a good harvest. Without them, our flowers would never turn into fruit.

**PLANTS TO ATTRACT POLLINATING INSECTS**

· Carnations

· Chamomile

· Chives

· Dill

· Goldenrod

· Hyssop

· Lavender
  (its flowers are ideal for harvesting and drying)

· Nasturtiums

· Pansies

· Sage

· Sunflowers

· Thyme

 Laurie's tips

• Some plants (mint, chives, raspberries) are invasive. It's better to plant them in containers rather than in the ground so they don't spread too much.

• Powdered eggshells make an excellent fertilizer for tomatoes and other plants. Stir small quantities into the soil at the base of your plants to make them beautiful and healthy.

*Chapter 5*

# BEAUTY
# &
# HEALTH

"THE MORE YOU KNOW,
THE LESS YOU NEED."

———————

Yvon Chouinard,
founder of Patagonia

# Spotlight on the cosmetics industry

The bathroom is a major clutter hotspot: cleaning supplies; products for body, hair, dental hygiene; samples; makeup; medicines, etc. So much stuff — especially given the often small space in this room. And most of these products contain fragrances, butane, toluene, parabens, heavy metals, and other chemical ingredients that, as you know, are harmful for our health as well as that of our planet.

### Why focus on these products?

The skin is our body's largest organ. It excretes toxins, but it also absorbs everything we put on it. So it's important to know what's in your creams and lotions, because some of the ingredients can build up in our systems, creating a whole host of undesirable effects (asthma, allergies, disrupted hormones, cancer, etc.). Even though cosmetics are partially regulated by Health Canada, some ingredients are not, and they do not have to be listed. And let's be honest, who among us, apart from chemists, really understands these notorious ingredient lists?

We vastly prefer using products that are as natural as possible to limit our exposure to chemical ingredients and other unknowns. Better still, we make our own body products and cosmetics. This means we know exactly what's in them, and we can customize them to suit our tastes.

Cosmetic products usually come in packaging that is not environmentally friendly. If we're paying attention to the containers in our kitchens, why not do the same in the bathroom? We don't often talk about the environmental impact of these containers, but they are just as polluting, and they end up contaminating soil and water once they become trash. So wherever possible, support companies that offer refills of their products. You will reduce the environmental impact of your beauty products.

### Real life according to Laurie

• The most ecological and healthy choice is, of course, to go without makeup entirely, but since we like to glam up once in a while we opt for more natural cosmetics and keep our makeup bags uncluttered. There's no need for ten different eye shadows if you're only going to wear it a few times a year.

• If you aren't interested in making your own beauty products, opt for companies that offer natural products without many additives. Zero-waste stores stock several refillable products. You can try them in small quantities and see which ones you like.

## Selling an image of perfection

Take a moment to observe the next cosmetics ads you see, and their implied promise of happiness. Cosmetics companies spend vast sums of money to make us buy their products by exploiting our weakness for marketing targeted at our supposed imperfections. Their goal is to make us dream of more beautiful skin, a more glowing complexion, goddess-like hair ...

Although the cosmetics industry wants us to find happiness in a miracle cream, it's important to ask: Would a beauty routine using a dozen different products really make me happier? For us, the answer is obvious: Simplicity is the best way, and if we can save time and money at the same time, all the better. So we opt for simple, multipurpose products that every member of the family can use. This also has the fantastic side benefit of creating more space on our shelves.

Over the next few pages, we'll show you how to make your own beauty and hygiene products, and give you the tools to make your own bathroom more minimalist. You'll also find ways to reduce your water consumption, because the bathroom is a wasteful room.

# Our favourite recipes

## LIP BALM

You will need:

Double boiler

Scale

5 empty lip balm tubes with lids

4 g beeswax

5 g coconut oil

3 g shea butter

8 g sweet almond oil

OPTIONAL: essential oils of your choice (mint, orange, lavender, etc.)

1. Clean and sterilize your pots, utensils, and containers.

2. Weigh out all of the ingredients and place in the top of a double boiler.

3. Place the double boiler over low heat. Heat the mixture, stirring occasionally, until the wax is melted and fully combined with the other ingredients.

4. Carefully pour the mixture into the tubes. Allow the balm to set before capping.

## MAKEUP-REMOVING OIL

Oil is ideal for removing makeup without irritating the skin. Place a few drops on your fingertips and rub over your whole face before rinsing with a cloth soaked in hot water. Repeat several times until there are no traces of makeup on the cloth.

If your skin is prone to acne, some oils are more comedogenic than others, so choose one for your skin type. We like jojoba oil.

Fill an amber glass bottle with the oil of your choice and keep it out of direct light.

**BODY BUTTER**

This recipe contains three interchangeable ingredients. You can, for example, use olive or grapeseed oil to replace coconut or sweet almond oil, or switch the shea butter out for cocoa butter.

You will need:

Double boiler

Shallow glass airtight container with a lid

½ cup (125 ml) shea butter
This nourishing butter is perfect for hydrating and protecting the skin against winter dryness.

¼ cup (60 ml) sweet almond oil
This hydrating, soothing oil has antioxidant properties.

¼ cup (60 ml) coconut oil
This oil is rapidly absorbed by the skin. It contains vitamins A and E, which help the skin regenerate.

15 to 30 drops of essential oil of your choice
A few top combinations: lavender/orange, ylang-ylang/vanilla, geranium/grapefruit.

1. Clean and sterilize your pots, utensils, and container.

2. Place the shea butter, sweet almond oil, and coconut oil in the top of a double boiler.

3. Place the double boiler over low heat. Heat the mixture, stirring often, until the shea butter is perfectly melted and ingredients are fully combined.

4. Remove the pan from the heat and stir in the essential oils. Let cool, and then transfer to the fridge and chill for an hour.

5. Using an electric mixer, whip the chilled mixture for several minutes, until the texture becomes airy. Scoop it into your airtight container to store.

NOTE: Do not add essential oils if you are pregnant or if the body butter will be used by young children. Certain oils (lemon, grapefruit, bergamot, mandarin) increase photosensitivity, so if you use one of these oils, avoid exposure to sunlight for 6 hours after applying the butter.

 Laurie's tip

We used this butter as part of our "anti-stretch mark" routines during pregnancy. We modified the recipe slightly: ½ cup (125 ml) shea butter, ¼ cup (60 ml) cocoa butter, and ¼ cup (60 ml) sweet almond oil.

Our skin is covered in (good) bacteria that, among other things, are responsible for the smell created when they come into contact with armpit sweat. Because each person is as unique as the bacteria that live on them, we tested a plethora of natural deodorant recipes before finding one that suited us. A recipe that works for one person can be disastrous for another.

Here we suggest two deodorant recipes — tested and approved, simple and effective — that you can make at home. One is a spray, and the other is a more traditional stick deodorant.

## SPRAY

You will need:

Small funnel

1 oz (30 ml) spray bottle

Vodka or flower water of your choice

25 drops of palmarosa essential oil

10 drops of tea tree oil

Essential oil of your choice
(geranium, lavender, sandalwood,
patchouli, etc.)

1. Clean and sterilize your utensils and containers.

2. Use the funnel to fill the spray bottle with vodka.

3. Add essential oils. Cap and shake well.

4. Shake before using and spray on armpits.

NOTES: This recipe is very similar to a perfume, so choose essential oils you like.

Apply as needed during the day. Be aware of any irritation caused by the alcohol.

## STICK

You will need:

Scale

Double boiler

Empty deodorant sticks

15 g coconut oil

15 g shea butter

8 g soy wax

20 g arrowroot powder or cornstarch

12 g aluminum-free baking soda

10 g zinc oxide

10 drops of essential oil of your
choice (palmarosa, tea tree, etc.)

1. Clean and sterilize your pots, utensils, and containers.

2. Weigh out the coconut oil, shea butter, and soy wax and place in the top of a double boiler.

3. Place the double boiler over low heat. Heat the mixture, stirring often, until it is perfectly melted and fully combined.

4. Remove the pan from the heat and let cool for a couple of minutes. Stir in the remaining ingredients.

5. Carefully pour the mixture into the empty deodorant sticks. Allow the mixture to set for at least 24 hours before capping.

NOTE: For sensitive skin, substitute white clay for the baking soda.

## ROLL-ON PERFUME

Pour a neutral oil (such as sweet almond) into a roll-on container and add essentials oils of your choice. Here are some of the blends we love.

· Relaxing
  15 drops of lavender essential oil
  10 drops of mandarin essential oil

· Romantic
  15 drops of rose essential oil
  10 drops of bergamot essential oil

· Reviving
  15 drops of orange essential oil
  5 drops of rosemary essential oil

· Woodsy
  15 drops of balsam fir or Scots pine essential oil
  5 drops of eucalyptus oil

· Floral
  15 drops of neroli essential oil
  10 drops of ylang-ylang essential oil

Roll onto pulse points, in other words the places where you give off most heat (wrists, behind the ears, elbow creases). Be careful: Citrus essential oils increase photosensitivity, so do not apply before sun exposure.

## COFFEE SCRUB

This recipe is perfect for using up your morning coffee grounds. The coffee acts as an exfoliant as well as stimulates your circulation. It's also an effective treatment against cellulite. Makes one treatment.

You will need:

½ cup (125 ml) coffee grounds

½ cup (125 ml) granulated sugar for a coarser scrub or powdered sugar for gentler exfoliation

¼ cup (60 ml) sweet almond or coconut oil

3 tsp (15 ml) sea salt

2 or 3 drops of essential oil of your choice for scent (sweet orange, ylang-ylang, or vanilla)

1. Clean and sterilize your utensils and container.

2. Combine all of the ingredients in a bowl and stir well.

3. Apply to the body in circular motions. Beware: This is messy! But afterward you'll have skin as soft as a baby's bottom.

## SUGAR AND HONEY LIP EXFOLIANT

A quick and easy recipe to exfoliate your lips naturally and hydrate them gently. Perfect for the winter, when temperature changes can dry out our lips.

You will need:

Small airtight glass jar

2 tsp (10 ml) brown sugar

1 tsp (5 ml) liquid honey

1 tsp (5 ml) oil of your choice (coconut, almond, olive, etc.)

1. Clean and sterilize your utensils and container.

2. Combine all of the ingredients in a small bowl and stir well. Transfer to the glass jar.

3. Apply to lips, rubbing gently. Rinse with warm or hot water. Your lips will be naturally moisturized and kissable.

## Hair products

One of the important points to note about simplicity and minimalism is accepting our bodies and the way we naturally are. This includes our hair. Embrace your natural colour and texture, or opt for more environmentally friendly dyes and gentle products for your hair and scalp.

Washing your hair less often is another way of saving large amounts of time and water. However, if you haven't yet switched over to the "no poo" method (giving up washing your hair and letting its natural oils hydrate it instead), shampoo bars are a good option. They come without packaging and are now available for all types of hair. Be patient if you haven't yet found the one that works for you.

### Real life according to Laurie

Both of us have opted for highlights instead of colouring all our hair. Highlights require less maintenance, and we ask our hairdresser not to start too close to the root for a more natural look.

Check if your hairdresser is part of the Green Circle Salons network, which collects hair, dye containers, and other hairdressing materials to give them a second life and divert them from landfills.

## DRY SHAMPOO

This recipe for dry shampoo will help you wash your hair less often. It's perfect for quickly freshening up your mane.

You will need:

Salt shaker or small jar with a lid

5 tsp (25 ml) cornstarch

2 tsp (10 ml) white clay

5 drops of lavender essential oil

5 drops of mint essential oil

1. Clean and sterilize your utensils and containers.

2. Combine all of the ingredients in a small bowl and stir well. Transfer to a salt shaker to sprinkle on your hair as needed. You can also store it in a small jar and apply it with a makeup brush you no longer use.

3. After applying to hair, leave to act for several minutes, then brush hair to distribute the shampoo.

## APPLE CIDER VINEGAR RINSE

There's nothing better than this rinse to give you soft hair and rebalance your scalp's bacterial flora. Extremely simple to make, it will bring the shine back to your hair.

You will need:

4-cup (1-L) Mason jar

3 tbsp (45 ml) apple cider vinegar

Water

1. Clean and sterilize your container.

2. Add the apple cider vinegar to the Mason jar, and then fill jar with water.

3. In the shower, pour the mixture over freshly washed hair, wait a few minutes, and rinse with cold water.

4. Brush and dry as normal.

## FACE LOTION

This lotion is perfect for customizing according to your needs and skin type. As with our other recipes, the ingredients are interchangeable (jojoba oil, olive oil, etc.), so use whatever you have on hand.

You will need:

Electric mixer

Scale

Double boiler

Electric mixer

**FOR THE OIL MIXTURE**

30 g jojoba oil (or argan, olive, or coconut oil, depending on your skin type)

5.6 g emulsifying wax (Olivem 1000 or vegetable emulsifying wax)

**FOR THE WATER MIXTURE**

16.6 g aloe gel

1.3 g vegetable glycerine

40 g rose water (or Labrador tea, or lavender or neroli essential oil, depending on your skin type)

**ADDITIVES**

5 drops of vitamin E oil

12 drops of essential oils of your choice (lavender, rose, tea tree, or cedar, depending on your skin type)

*Recipe courtesy Marise Pitre, aromatherapy adviser at Hunzaroma.*

1. Clean and sterilize your pots, utensils, and container.

2. For the oil mixture: Weigh out the jojoba oil and emulsifying wax, and place in the top of a double boiler. Place the double boiler over low heat. Heat the mixture, stirring often, until the wax is perfectly melted and ingredients are fully combined.

3. For the water mixture: Weigh out the aloe gel, vegetable glycerine, and rose water, and place in the top of a double boiler. Place the double boiler over low heat. Heat the mixture, stirring often, until the ingredients are fully combined.

4. Using an electric mixer, whip the oil mixture for 5 to 10 seconds, and then let sit for 5 minutes.

5. Add the water mixture to the oil mixture, and whip for 10 more seconds. Pause and then beat again until well emulsified (the mixture will become whiter and the texture will appear more whipped).

6. Transfer to the fridge to cool completely.

7. Once cool, add the vitamin E and essential oils. Stir well.

8. Transfer to airtight containers and store in the fridge.

NOTE: This will keep for several months in the fridge, so take out small amounts as needed.

# Purging the medicine cabinet

To start, go through your bathroom with a fine-tooth comb and see what you can declutter. Empty out the cupboards and drawers, and look at everything you own. Check the expiry dates and dispose of anything unusable in an appropriate place (for example, return expired medicines to a pharmacy; *do not* throw them down the toilet or into the garbage). Put aside anything you no longer use or use only rarely. Pass these items along to someone else or give them to institutions that need them. Don't keep anything you only use a few times a year. As we have already seen in the chapter on cleaning, you can use the same cleaning products in both the kitchen and the bathroom because they have multiple uses. In the end, you will have more space under the sink, and will reduce your exposure to chemical products. Most importantly, don't throw out all of your products right away. Finish them up before you replace them with more natural ones.

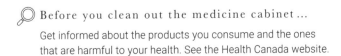

Before you clean out the medicine cabinet...

Get informed about the products you consume and the ones that are harmful to your health. See the Health Canada website.

## Essential oils

We have fallen completely under the spell of essential oils. Discovering them was, in part, the trigger for our green journey. We diffuse them, use them in cosmetics and cleaning products, and even for minor illnesses (sore throat, cold, congestion, etc.) on a daily basis. They are made from plant extracts and are extremely potent and highly scented. They must be used with care.

We like essential oils for their effectiveness and because each one has its own properties (reviving, energizing, relaxing, calming, etc.).

**OILS TO HAVE IN YOUR HOME PHARMACY**

· Lavender
Repels mosquitoes and headlice, treats burns, relaxes

· Tea tree
Antibacterial, anti-blemish

· Lemon
Antiseptic, degreaser

· Peppermint
Deodorizing, good for digestive issues, painkiller

· Palmarosa
Antibacterial

· Eucalyptus
Decongestant, mosquito repellent

· Ravintsara
Boosts immune system, antiviral

## WHAT OILS TO USE FOR EACH SKIN TYPE

· Oily skin
Tea tree, lavender, cedar, rose geranium, palmarosa

· Dry skin
Neroli, rose

· Sensitive skin
Chamomile, lavender

· Mature skin
Rose, rose geranium, rosewood

## WHICH FLOWER WATER TO USE FOR EACH SKIN TYPE

Flower waters are an excellent replacement for commercial tonic water and can also be used as perfume. These have the same properties as essential oils but are less concentrated.

· Oily skin
Rosemary, lavender, geranium

· Dry skin
Neroli, rose

· Sensitive skin
Chamomile, rose

· Mature skin
Rose, geranium, neroli, cornflower

NOTE: Consult an aromatherapist for more advice on how to use certain oils. We both have an essential oils bible at home to guide us in their use and application.

## Our skincare routines

Having a simple skincare routine gives us more time and minimizes the number of products we own, because most of them are made from ingredients in the pantry.

**MORNING**

- Clean face with makeup-removing oil, rinse off with a cloth and hot water.
- Spray flower water all over face.
- Apply lotion all over the face, neck, and décolletage.

**EVENING**

- To remove eye makeup, warm a small amount of coconut oil between your fingers and gently rub over eyes. Then use a washable cotton pad dampened with hot water to wipe away all makeup residue.
- For the face, massage makeup-removing oil (see page 163) all over, then wipe away with a cloth dampened with hot water.
- Once the skin is clean, spray your face with flower water (for your skin type; see page 179) and apply face lotion (see page 174) to face, neck, and décolletage.
- If necessary, apply tea tree oil to dry out blemishes.
- Apply a thick layer of lip balm at bedtime so that lips are perfectly hydrated when you wake up.

- We like to gently exfoliate our skin with a paste of baking soda and water, or a mixture of honey and powdered sugar. Massage onto face for a gentle face mask.

- Once the skin is well exfoliated, it's the perfect time to apply a home-made clay beauty mask (white or pink for sensitive and mature skin, green for oily skin) or spread a generous layer of honey over skin and leave for 10 minutes. Clay is purifying, and perfect when the skin flares up. Honey nourishes the skin, and its antibacterial and anti-inflammatory properties are effective at helping blemishes to scar over. Be sure to choose organic honey so you are not applying pesticides to your skin.

- For the body, we also exfoliate occasionally with our coffee scrub (see page 170). Then we moisturize with our whipped body butter (see page 164). Soft skin guaranteed!

 Laurie's tip

Soak your cloths and washable cotton pads in a mixture
of hot water and sodium percarbonate to make them white again.

# Disposable
# or reusable items

Here are a few examples of polluting bathroom items that are easy to replace with a more environmentally friendly counterpart.

- Disposable makeup-removing wipes
  Fabric washcloths
- Disposable cotton makeup-removing pads
  Washable cotton pads or wipes
- Disposable razors
  Safety razors with a blade
- Cotton swabs
  Steel oriculi
- Bottled shampoo
  Shampoo bar or bulk refillable shampoo
- Shower gel
  Bar soap
- Plastic toothbrush
  Bamboo toothbrush
- Toothpaste tube
  Bulk toothpaste
- Dental floss
  Floss in a refillable container

NOTE: To this list we could also add washable handkerchiefs and toilet paper, as well as menstrual cups and other reusable sanitary products, but we are aware that this is another step. Go at your own pace.

# A note on
# water consumption

Water is an essential resource for life on Earth. Proof: Our bodies are around 60% water. However, in just a few years, it's estimated that more than half of the planet will be feeling the stress of imminent shortages.

In the bathroom, the shower, toilet, and bath are all a major part of our drinking-water consumption. However, we can all make some efforts to reduce our usage on a daily basis.

If you keep future generations in mind, saving water should be easy!

**TIPS TO REDUCE
WATER CONSUMPTION**

- Take shorter showers.
- Install a water-saving shower head.
- Collect water.
  Put a bucket under the shower, over the drain, to collect the water. You can use it to water plants or flush the toilet.
  Very economical!
- Put a brick in the toilet tank to reduce its water consumption by 1.5 L each flush.
- When you buy a new toilet, opt for a more environmentally friendly model.

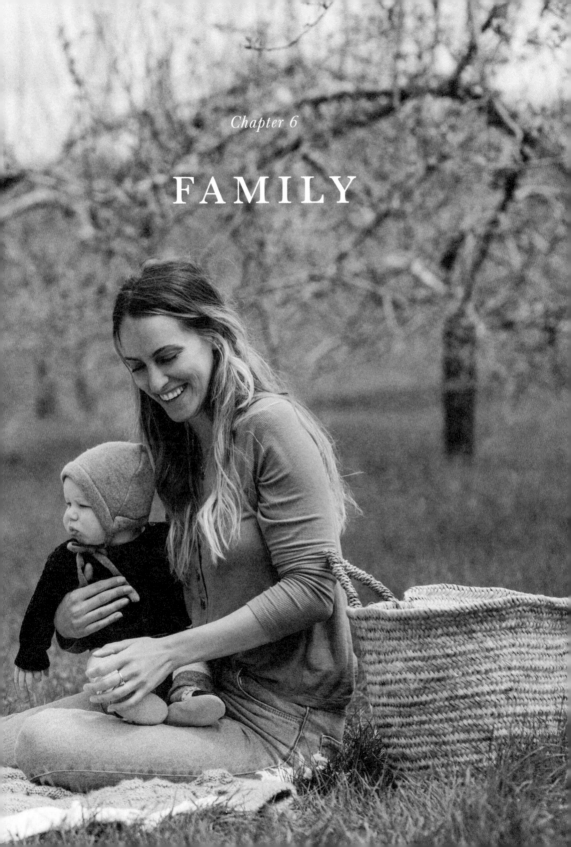

Chapter 6

# FAMILY

"CHILDREN DON'T NEED MORE THINGS. THE BEST TOY A CHILD CAN HAVE IS A PARENT WHO GETS DOWN ON THE FLOOR AND PLAYS WITH THEM."

Bruce Perry, M.D., Ph.D.

# Embracing minimalism as a family

It's impossible not to talk about family and children when you're dealing with subjects like the environment and minimalism. Having a family can make these issues quite challenging.

Our children have certainly changed our lives for the better. However, becoming a parent brings its share of joy, learning, worries, and … stuff! Kid stores are overflowing with objects and toys for little ones, as appealing to the parents as they are to each child. As parents, we used to often make impulsive purchases stemming from our overflowing love for our children. Never mind everything they received from grandparents, uncles, aunts, and friends on birthdays and holidays. You can imagine our pain at becoming cluttered once again after spending all that time decluttering our homes.

After we had our baby showers, we realized that the lists of baby essentials online were long and overwhelming. It's easy to get discouraged by everything you're supposed to acquire to welcome a new little person into the world. This is the reason why some people say that choosing to have children is an environmentally harmful act, explaining that the carbon footprint of each new individual (especially in the West) causes substantially more pollution on our already overpopulated planet.

Let's modify this extremist eco-militant idea. We believe that it is possible to have children and to educate them so that they become responsible citizens. One ignorant person pollutes as much as, if not more than, several informed people put together!

To sum up, we try to transmit values to our children that are in harmony with nature, teach them that happiness can't be found in material possessions, and educate them to take care of the Earth in their daily actions.

# Reducing
# our children's
# carbon footprint

Giving birth to a baby makes you question a lot of things. It goes without saying that we want the best for our children and future generations. We want them to have the chance to see nature the way we did (before it was covered in tons of plastic waste), to swim in the ocean, have access to drinking water, and have a good quality of life without the threat of natural catastrophes, pollution-related illnesses, smog, or the disappearance of the ozone layer. So what can we do to reduce our children's carbon footprints and show them how to care for this already fragile ecosystem?

To start, by inculcating in them the same zero-waste rules we adults have. In other words: refuse, reduce, reuse, recycle, rot.

Living simply as a family means consuming less and spending more time together, choosing human relationships over material goods. It implies fewer purchases, and less time working to pay for them. Take 2 minutes to think about the following question: Are our fondest childhood memories associated with material possessions or family moments? The answer will give you a clue as to how to live in harmony with the world around you.

# Limiting consumption as a family

### Buy less, buy better

When you have your first baby, it's easy to get carried away buying adorable little outfits, toys, and other gadgets that at the time seem to be totally necessary. But ask the parents you know what was most useful to them when their kids were little, and draw up your list based on these answers. Of course, every child is different, and every child has their own needs, but corporate marketing is highly skilled at playing with our emotions and convincing us that we need to buy everything in order to be better parents. Be attuned to all the commercialization surrounding anything related to parenthood.

Tell your friends and family about your approach and your real needs so you don't end up receiving tons of clothes and toys that will gather dust in the cupboards. Make a list and give it to people: They will be happy giving you something that you will genuinely find useful. If they insist on buying you something new, encourage them to buy from local creators and traders — a great way to support the local economy!

For older children, ask for experiences instead of material goods for holidays and birthdays. Experiences will leave longer-lasting memories and allow the giver to spend quality time with your children. Also, opt to give and receive homemade presents. Set an example by making bath salts for granny with your children. Children love creating and giving, so always suggest homemade gift ideas instead of rushing off to the mall to track down the perfect present.

### Caution

Flame retardants can be found in several products for children (car seats, mattresses, carpets, even pyjamas). As the name indicates, these chemicals prevent fire from spreading, but they also contain volatile compounds that disrupt the endocrine system in children and pregnant women. We prefer to avoid them.

## Our baby essentials

Here is our list of essentials, tried and tested, for a first baby. Of course, you can add things to the list according to your own situation, but these are the items from our plunge into motherhood that we consider indispensable.

- Car seat
- A good stroller that meets your needs
- High-quality baby carrier or sling
- Easy-clean high chair
- Crib
- Organic soy foam mattress and organic cotton sheet
- A few muslin blankets
- Two quilts for diaper changing
- Washable diapers
- A few non-toxic disposable diapers for the early days
- Washable gentle wipes
- Neutral massage oil (sweet almond, apricot, coconut, calendula, etc.)
- A few organic cotton pyjamas
- Knitted booties and hats
- A few comfortable outfits that are easy to put on (we especially like harem pants with very wide waistbands that can grow with your baby for several months)
- Baby playmat gym (can be acquired later)
- Baby bouncer or vibrating chair
- A notebook to record all those wonderful moments

NOTE: All these items can be bought used except for car seats, which for safety reasons should be bought new.

### A note on car seats

We both chose a car seat from the company Nuna, which sells organic cotton seats without flame retardants. When we have finished using the seat, we will be able to take it to a depot listed on the CAA website. The CAA in Quebec is part of a recycling program to give car seats a second life. The plastic is used to make park benches, and the straps can be turned into harnesses and other products for animals. Check out https://recycleyourcarseat.org/where-do-i -recycle-my-seat/ for more information on recycling programs in Canada and the U.S.

### A note on slings and baby carriers

There are two main types of baby carriers: wrap style or structured. The wrap style is great for those first few weeks with the baby, who will want to be attached to you all the time. As the baby grows, a more structured style that can carry up to 45 pounds will be more suitable for their weight. When we have our baby in a carrier, they can see and discover the world from our eye level, which increases their feeling of proximity. Take your time to weigh all your options in specialist baby stores, and choose a carrier according to what you want to use it for and your (and your partner's, as applicable) body type.

## Buy used

Children grow really fast, so there's no need to buy too much stuff in advance, and it's smarter to opt for used items. You can find everything second-hand (stroller, high chair, clothes, etc.). You'll save huge amounts of money and still end up with clothes and equipment that are nearly new. It's not rare for a baby to wear something for just a few months before the clothing gets too small. You can find beautiful pieces in excellent condition in thrift stores or online marketplaces. Just be careful not to fall into the trap of buying more than you need. You will end up with too much clutter and feel as though you're back at square one. The same goes for toys. Children quickly get bored with their toys, so don't spend huge sums to get the latest must-haves. Try to find what you want used, and sell things when your child no longer uses them. This way another family will be able to benefit from the items.

And lastly, share! Ask around: You will no doubt have friends who want to get rid of clothes or toys that their children are too big for, and vice versa.

 Caution

We love vintage toys! But be cautious of painted toys, because paint often used to contain lead. We don't want children putting heavy metals in their mouths.

## Reuse and repair

Think long term when you make purchases. We recommend choosing quality items so that they last longer and can be passed on to another child. For this reason, we favour neutral, unisex colours that don't go out of style. We also like clothes made from organic natural fibres (cotton, hemp, bamboo, linen), which are renewable resources and more comfortable than synthetic fibres. Avoid plastic toys, which are less durable than wooden ones, and sometimes contain BPA, which can affect your child's development.

Try to repair clothes instead of throwing them away. This goes for toys and any other broken accessories, too, which can often be easily repaired instead of replaced. Include your children in the repair process, because this helps them learn to take care of their things.

It's a good idea to declutter the playroom or the child's bedroom from time to time. Here, too, encourage the child to help out: In this way, the child will notice the toys they no longer use, and can decide to give some away or sell them to make room for new ones. We like to say that for every object that comes into the house, another one has to leave.

### Laurie's tip

After washing, dry children's clothes on a clotheshorse rather than in the dryer to make them last longer and save on electricity. There's no need to wash clothes every time they are worn if they are still clean.

## Washable wipes

In our opinion, washable wipes are the easiest environmentally friendly switch to make. Just like disposable diapers, disposable wipes are highly polluting and contain perfumes and other products that can irritate the baby's bum. We recommend using simple wipes that can be washed along with the diapers. At diaper changes, spray the baby's bottom with a homemade mixture of water and gentle soap, then wipe with a washable wipe. When the wipe is dirty, put it with the used diapers to wait for the next wash. When you go out, put a few pre-moistened wipes in a small waterproof bag (be sure to bring another bag to put the used ones into).

## Soothers and bottles

It's better not to buy these items in advance, for the simple reason that every baby is different. There are tons of soothers on the market, but your baby might like just one brand. The same thing goes for bottle teats if you go the bottle-feeding route. Just test one kind of bottle to begin with to see if your baby takes to it.

Since they are going straight into babies' mouths, it's also advisable to choose natural rubber nipples.

### Those cloth diapers...

Cloth diapers are easier to use than they might seem and are way more environmentally friendly than disposable diapers. A single child uses between 5,000 and 8,000 disposable diapers before being potty trained. These diapers take 500 years to decompose! Do the math. Incredible quantities of diapers are found at landfill sites, and their production requires a great deal of water and resources.

In addition, disposable diapers contain a whole host of chemical ingredients to make them more absorbent (polymers and plastics). These toxic products will be in direct contact with your baby's delicate skin, which can cause irritations and other skin issues. All things considered, even though cloth diapers need to be washed regularly, they are far less polluting than disposable diapers.

Although they cost more upfront to buy, your initial investment will be quickly repaid, and you can even sell them when your baby is toilet trained. Or you can buy a used batch, which is what we did. Simply disinfect them thoroughly and give them a good scrubbing with a suitable product, which you will find in most children's stores. Several cities offer a rebate if you buy cloth diapers. Buying twenty or so should be plenty. You will need to wash them two or three times a week, but if you incorporate them into your laundry routine you will find that it isn't too complicated. And don't worry, cloth diapers have changed a lot since our grandmothers' days. Some companies even launder the diapers themselves and deliver them to your house. This is a very appealing option, although more expensive, for those who don't want to do the laundry at home.

### Real life according to Laurie

We still keep a few disposable diapers in our changing bags when we go out, but we opt for more environmentally friendly brands such as Parasol, The Honest Company, or Attitude Living. We also used disposables for the first few weeks of our babies' lives, which allowed us to rest and adapt to our new life! Newborns are often too small to wear one-size cloth diapers, and need newborn-sized ones, which is an extra investment for just a short period.

# The green nursery

We like to know what goes into every product that we put on our children's skins. This is the reason — along with the fact that we enjoy it — that we make the majority of products ourselves. By choosing homemade, we can keep their soft, delicate skin from absorbing various chemicals and perfumes. We make most of our baby products, and choose products with the most natural ingredients possible for anything we need to buy. For example, we use our body butter recipe without essential oils (see page 164) to moisturize baby's skin, because we prefer products that the whole family can use. After all, what's good for us is also good for them.

## Caution

Most of the recipes that follow contain essential oils. Although the use of essential oils in baby products is controversial, we assure you that we have used these recipes on our own children with no ill effects, and that they have been recommended by a certified aromatherapist. Do not substitute other oils in the recipes, because some can be harmful even though they are natural.

## Real life according to Laurie

Sometimes we don't have the time to make — or feel like making — these products. The good news is that many wonderful local companies make natural products for children, which sometimes are even sold in bulk.

# Our favourite recipes

This baby spray is economical, ecological, and non-toxic for babies' bums. You can also tuck a bottle into your changing bag, along with some wipes, to clean off your little munchkin's hands when you're out and about.

You will need:

3.4-oz (100-ml) spray bottle

1 tsp Castile soap or other gentle, perfume-free soap

Water

1. Put the soap in the spray bottle.

2. Fill the bottle with water.

3. Shake well before using.

**HOMEMADE MASSAGE OIL**

This massage oil is good for the whole family. Use it to give baby a relaxing massage after a bath, or Mom and Dad can rub it on their own stiff shoulders.

If you don't have all the ingredients on hand, don't panic! Simply use the vegetable oil of your choice.

You will need:

3.4-oz (100-ml) small amber glass bottle with a cap

3 tbsp + 1 tsp (50 ml) vegetable oil (almond, apricot, coconut, calendula, etc.)

5 drops of lavender essential oil

2 drops of Roman chamomile essential oil

Place all of the ingredients in the bottle and shake well.

NOTE: Avoid nut oils in case of allergy.

## SLEEPYTIME BLEND

We have included massage in our babies' bedtime routines right from birth. Massage has several benefits, including creating a bond, helping the child's development, promoting sleep and relaxation, etc. It's a lovely moment to share between baby and parent.

This gentle essential oil blend for babies and children is best massaged on the solar plexus just before naptime or bedtime. Massage with a small quantity.

You will need:

½-oz (15-ml) glass bottle with a cap (an empty, clean essential oil bottle works well)

1 ¼ tsp (6 ml) organic olive oil

100 drops mandarin or sweet orange essential oil

75 drops lavender essential oil

50 drops noble chamomile essential oil

1. Place all the ingredients in the bottle and shake well.

2. To use, apply 5 drops of the blend on baby's chest or spinal column and massage onto skin.

NOTE: Noble chamomile is effective but expensive. If you choose not to include it in the blend, simply add an equal amount of lavender or mandarin essential oil instead.

*Recipe courtesy Marise Pitre,*
*aromatherapy adviser at Hunzaroma.*

## BABY BOTTOM BALM

Super easy to make, economic, and efficient, this soothing balm is ideal for hydrating baby's delicate skin. We use it to prevent or treat diaper irritations.

This balm is also compatible with cloth diapers because it contains clay, not zinc. However, if you are applying it liberally to baby's bottom, put a disposable liner in the cloth diaper so the coconut oil doesn't leave an oily stain on the fabric.

You will need:

Shallow glass container with a lid

½ cup (125 ml) shea butter

3 tbsp (45 ml) coconut oil

1 tsp (5 ml) beeswax or candelilla

3 tbsp (45 ml) bentonite or white clay

5 drops of lavender essential oil

5 drops of tea tree oil

1. Place the shea butter, coconut oil, and beeswax in the top of a double boiler.

2. Place the double boiler over low heat. Heat the mixture, stirring occasionally, until the wax is melted and fully combined with the other ingredients.

3. Remove the pan from the heat. Let the pan cool slightly before refrigerating the mixture for about 30 minutes or until lightly solidified.

4. Using a hand whisk, beat in the bentonite and essential oils, whisking continuously until the mixture reaches a whipped consistency.

5. Transfer the finished balm to your container.

## TEETHING OIL

St. John's wort oil has analgesic properties that can help lessen babies' teething pain.

You will need:

½-oz (15-ml) glass bottle with a cap or a glass dropper (an empty, clean essential oil bottle works well)

25 drops of noble chamomile essential oil

3 tbsp (45 ml) St. John's wort oil

1. Place the noble chamomile essential oil and St. John's wort oil in the bottle and shake well.

2. To use, put 2 drops of the oil on a clean finger and massage onto baby's sore gums. Repeat once or twice at 5-minute intervals, two or three times a day.

Use for up to a week.

*Recipe courtesy Marise Pitre, aromatherapy adviser at Hunzaroma.*

## ANTISEPTIC HEALING BALM
## FOR THE WHOLE FAMILY

A natural balm to apply to cuts, scrapes, and other little booboos.

You will need:

Scale

Dark glass container with a lid

9 g beeswax

35 g sweet almond oil

35 g calendula oil

4 g zinc oxide

60 drops of tea tree oil

60 drops of lavender essential oil

25 drops of vitamin E oil

1. Weigh out the beeswax, almond oil, calendula oil, and zinc oxide and place in the top of a double boiler.

2. Place the double boiler over low heat. Heat the mixture, stirring occasionally, until the wax is melted and fully combined with the other ingredients.

3. Remove the pan from the heat and let cool for about 2 minutes. Add the essential oils and vitamin E, and stir well.

4. Transfer the finished balm to the container. It will keep for more than a year in a cool, dark place.

*Recipe courtesy Marise Pitre,*
*aromatherapy adviser at Hunzaroma.*

FAMILY

# Teaching children to care for the environment

*"We could never have loved the earth so well if we had had no childhood in it."*
– George Eliot

The most important thing we can do is transmit a love of nature to our children — this link is crucial for inspiring them to take care of the environment. The best way to engender respect for the planet in our little ones is to spend as much time as possible outside and familiarize them with the natural world.

Playing outside and enjoying nature has a whole host of benefits. Not only is it good for our physical and mental health, but being outside also brings us into contact with the environment around us and significantly reduces our — and our children's — stress levels. Some people even call this a dose of nature vitamin N! So go for a stroll in the forest, wander the green trails, play sports as a family, have picnics, go camping … All of these outside activities will encourage your children to be more aware of the beauty of nature and the importance of preserving it. Let them explore and have their own experiences. All the best childhood memories are of playing freely outside without any structured activities.

You can also explain to your children why it's important to take care of nature for the good of the planet, without being alarmist. Children are already bombarded with negative information about the environment. As well as increasing their stress levels, such an approach can give the impression that it's too late to do anything about it. Try instead to encourage them to find ways to reduce their impact, and guide them in their initiatives. It's never too late to teach good habits.

Above all, lead by example and be consistent in your own actions and deeds. Children learn a lot by copying, so be aware of your own role in their learning and development.

# Environmentally friendly family activities

Trust your children and let them go out to meet nature. From a very young age, children love simply going for a walk outside, exploring and discovering. Try not to intervene or direct their play unless there's something dangerous. Watch them: They know far more than we think, and often they show us what is important. Become a child once more and savour the scent of every flower you pass, and rediscover the joy of playing outside.

If you live according to your values and have a positive mindset, your children will absorb it. Be confident, even if you sometimes feel that your teachings are having no effect. One day they will surprise you!

Here are a few ways to reconnect with nature with your children. Adapt them according to age. The most important thing is to have fun. Try to limit your children's screen time and incorporate outside activity every day. This is a habit that can seem hard to develop at the beginning, but after a while you will be very glad you stuck with it.

1.
Make a garden. Children are amazed
by the process of growing fruits and
vegetables, and will be more aware
of their food as a result.

2.
Build a birdhouse or a bird feeder
so you can watch the birds and identify different local species.

3.
Start a nature notebook. Ask the
children to make notes, draw, or
photograph whatever they see in nature.

4.
Compost. As well as making a significant
reduction in the amount of waste you
produce, you will be able to teach your children about the natural cycles of food and
to use the compost in your garden.

5.
Go on a weekend camping trip.
There's nothing better for reconnecting
with nature than sleeping and eating
outside.

6.
Make and build things with
different items gathered from nature.

7.
Make wind chimes out of shells.

8.
Invent a recipe with food from
the garden that needs using up.

9.
Go and visit an animal sanctuary
so your children can learn more about
local wild animals.

10.
Go berry picking at an organic
farm in season. Freeze some for
your stores.

11.
Organize a neighbourhood clean-up.
When you're out for a walk, take gloves
and garbage bags, and pick up all the trash
you find. Your children will become more
conscientious about the principle of
leaving a place cleaner than you found it.

12.
Go skating. There are so many fantastic
outdoor skating rinks.

13.

Visit a beekeeper to learn more about bees and honey production.

14.

Make holiday decorations by baking ornaments that you can decorate.

15.

Explore the parks in your region.

16.

Make a map of the night sky and try to spot the different constellations.

17.

Dye your old clothes and sheets with natural dyes made from food (see page 46).

18.

Play around with modelling clay or homemade salt dough (see recipe on page 225).

19.

Get the children to take part in making their own zero-waste lunch. Packaged snacks are a major source of waste, and when multiplied by the number of children at school every day, the amount of packaging is truly disturbing. Get them to help you cook their favourite snacks and put them in small reusable bags to take to school.

20.

Protest for the planet. Take part in local citizens' initiatives as a family.

21.

Make a snowman in the winter.

22.

Enjoy having one electricity-free evening a month. Light candles and get out the board games. The kids will have fun and you will save on your electricity bill.

# Ideas for play

Select a few objects to hide in an opaque fabric bag. Help your children develop their sense of touch by trying to guess what objects are inside it.

This simple game doesn't require you to purchase anything.

**SALT DOUGH**

There's no need to buy commercial modelling dough when it's so easy to make your own! Small children just love playing with the dough and discovering textures, while older children enjoy creating shapes.

You will need:

2 cups (500 ml) all-purpose flour

1 cup (250 ml) fine salt

1 cup (250 ml) water

1. Combine all of the ingredients in a large bowl and mix well. Add a little oil to smooth out the dough, if necessary.

2. Colour your dough with natural ingredients, such as ground cinnamon, turmeric powder, beet juice, or a few drops of liquid chlorophyll.

## SEED BOMBS

Makes about 60 seed bombs

You will need:

4.5 lbs (2 kg) clay soil

Large handful of black earth

Handful of mixed flower seeds

1. Warm up the clay in your hands to make it more malleable, and then flatten it into a pancake on a hard surface (spreading earth on your work surface in advance will help keep the clay from sticking).

2. Sprinkle the black earth all over the clay pancake — just enough to cover it, but not too much, since you want the clay to remain a little sticky.

3. Sprinkle the flower seeds evenly over the surface of your clay and earth pancake.

4. Roll up the pancake as if making sushi. Cut the rolled pancake into ½-inch (1-cm) slices. Roll each slice in the palms of your hands to shape it into a small ball.

5. Let the balls dry for about two days.

6. Choose a spot where you'd like flowers to grow and then throw your ball on the ground. Choose a place where nobody will cut the grass, so you will be able to see your flowers. If doing this in early spring, wait for the ground to thaw so the flowers have a chance to survive.

NOTE: It's important to choose non-invasive species so you don't destroy your neighbourhood's ecological balance. Ideally, choose a local flower species. You can be even more environmentally friendly by choosing seeds for a pollinator garden that will attract birds and bees. You can also use herb seeds or even grass seeds.

# Children's parties

Children love themed parties and decorations. All too often, however, a birthday party means disposable plates, helium balloons, and loot bags.

**TIPS FOR MAKING YOUR PARTY
MORE ENVIRONMENTALLY FRIENDLY**

### DECORATIONS

- Choose decorations that can be used for other parties.
- Make wreaths and bunting from old sheets or sweaters.
- Choose a nature-related theme and gather wildflowers to decorate the table.
- Rent or borrow accessories instead of buying them.
- Use recycled paper to make the invitations.

### ACTIVITIES

- Bring out a box of costumes and props and let the children make up characters.
- Make salt dough (see page 225).
- Play outside if the weather allows. Organize a nature treasure hunt.

## Final note

Include the children! Ask them if they can think of good deeds they can do for the planet. Their answers might surprise you. It's important not to preach to those around you, but instead to show that being green is fun and interesting.

## THE TABLE

- Opt for a reusable tablecloth.
- Choose a menu with minimal washing up in mind (think nibbles and finger foods).
- Choose small cakes rather than one big one — there will be fewer dishes to wash and less waste.
- Cut up old sheets and clothes to make napkins for wiping little hands.
- Use reusable dishes.
- Give guests a pen to mark their own glasses.
- Stock up on candies and snacks at a bulk store. Set them out in glass dishes on the table.
- Choose fruit water instead of fruit juice. Simply add fresh fruit to a large jug of water.
- Opt for a vegetarian menu.

## GIFTS

- Resist the temptation to hand out loot bags.
- If you really want to give your guests something, consider a plant cutting or a seed bomb (see recipe on page 226).
- Ask that guests not bring gifts. This might seem over the top, but most of the time these presents are superfluous and unnecessary.
- Let your children know that the important thing is to spend time together and celebrate.
- Opt for a group gift: an outing, a class, etc.

*To our sons, August and Noah*

Our wish is for you to fall in love with nature and take care of it. May every second of your life be sprinkled with small joys, passion, and sweet moments. Thank you for opening our eyes to something bigger than us.

*Thank you to our partners, Nicolas and Benjamin*

Thank you for supporting us from the beginning of our adventure, for putting up with hearing the words "bag" and "zero waste" all day long, for bringing your reusable containers even if you sometimes feel embarrassed, and for doing your part with us. Thank you for your patience, and for looking after our bundles of joy during our numerous photo shoots. We could not do all this without you.

*Thank you to the teams at Parfum d'encre and Anansi for bringing this book to life. It was one of our dreams.*

And finally, thank you, the reader holding this book in your hands. It's thanks to you that all this exists. We don't have enough words to express all our gratitude toward everyone who has supported us since the beginning. Thank you for your support and for believing in change. The future of the planet is in your hands.

Follow us for more inspiration

danslesac.co
facebook.com/infodanslesac
instagram.com/dans_le_sac
pinterest.ca/danslesac
youtube.com/danslesac

Original edition published in French under the title *Minimal: Pour un mode de vie durable*, by Parfum d'encre, an imprint of Groupe d'édition la courte échelle inc.

Copyright © 2019 Les éditions Parfum d'encre
English translation copyright © 2021 J. C. Sutcliffe

Published in Canada in 2021 and the USA in 2021 by House of Anansi Press Inc.
www.houseofanansi.com

House of Anansi Press is committed to protecting our natural environment. This book is made of material from well-managed FSC®-certified forests, recycled materials, and other controlled sources.

House of Anansi Press is a Global Certified Accessible™ (GCA by Benetech) publisher. The ebook version of this book meets stringent accessibility standards and is available to students and readers with print disabilities.

25 24 23 22 21    1 2 3 4 5

Library and Archives Canada Cataloguing in Publication

Title: Minimal : for simple and sustainable living / Laurie Barrette, Stéphanie Mandréa ; translated by J. C. Sutcliffe.
Other titles: Minimal, pour un mode de vie durable. English Names: Barrette, Laurie, 1990– author. | Mandréa, Stéphanie, author. | Sutcliffe, J. C., translator.
Description: Translation of: Minimal, pour un mode de vie durable.
Identifiers: Canadiana (print) 20200367781 | Canadiana (ebook) 20200367862 | ISBN 9781487009434 (hardcover) | ISBN 9781487009441 (EPUB) | ISBN 9781487009458 (Kindle)
Subjects: LCSH: Sustainable living. | LCSH: Voluntary simplicity movement. | LCSH: Waste minimization.
Classification: LCC GE196 .B3713 2021 | DDC 640.28/6—dc23

First-edition publisher: Ann Châteauvert
Art direction: Julie Massy
Book design: Catherine Charbonneau
Photography: Stéphanie Mandréa
Typesetting: Marijke Friesen

*House of Anansi Press respectfully acknowledges that the land on which we operate is the Traditional Territory of many Nations, including the Anishinabeg, the Wendat, and the Haudenosaunee. It is also the Treaty Lands of the Mississaugas of the Credit.*

 Canada Council    Conseil des Arts
for the Arts    du Canada

 ONTARIO ARTS COUNCIL
CONSEIL DES ARTS DE L'ONTARIO
an Ontario government agency
un organisme du gouvernement de l'Ontario

FSC
www.fsc.org
MIX
Paper from
responsible sources
FSC® C011825

*We acknowledge for their financial support of our publishing program the Canada Council for the Arts, the Ontario Arts Council, and the Government of Canada.*

Printed and bound in Canada